A MERE REFLECTION OF MY MOTHER

A Mere Reflection *of* My Mother

ANNE ARBOR

A Mere Reflection of My Mother: A Memoir by Anne Arbor

© 2026 by Anne Arbor

All rights reserved. No portion of this publication may be reproduced, stored in a retrieval system, or transmitted by any means—electronic, mechanical, photocopying, recording, or any other—except for brief quotations in printed reviews, without the prior written permission of the publisher.

Library of Congress Control Number: 2025919617
ISBN: 978-1-964686-77-6 (paperback) 978-1-964686-78-3 (ebook)

This book is based on true events reflecting the author's memory of them. Some names and characteristics may have been changed, some events compressed, and some dialogue recreated.

Editors: Noëlla Simmons, Stephanie Thompson
Cover and Interior Design: Emma Elzinga

Printed in the United States of America
First Edition

3 West Garden Street, Ste. 718
Pensacola, FL 32502
www.indigoriverpublishing.com

Ordering Information:

Quantity sales: Special discounts are available on quantity purchases by corporations, associations, and others. For details, contact the publisher at the address above.

Orders by US trade bookstores and wholesalers: Please contact the publisher at the address above.

With Indigo River Publishing, you can always expect great books, strong voices, and meaningful messages. Most importantly, you'll always find . . . *words worth reading.*

*For my daughters, with so much love and gratitude
for the gift of being your mother.*

To my mother, may your spirit soar above the clouds.

1

January 1, 2011, was my fortieth birthday. Most people cringe at the thought of turning forty, but not me. Years of struggle and sacrifice had culminated, and it was now time to enjoy life. Turning forty marked my transition from struggling to thriving. With my much-adored twin three-year-old daughters, a long-term relationship, and a job that met my needs, I was comfortable. My basic needs were met. Two days prior to my birthday, my mother, Marion, celebrated her sixty-first.

We weren't close. I lived with her until I was four, and I can count the number of times I saw her since. Twenty times between the ages of four and ten, and seven times after that. Before I was old enough for kindergarten, she dropped me off with my father and pulled away in an old beat-up, rusted white pickup truck with Mitch behind the wheel—Mitch who eventually became her second husband and ultimately changed the trajectory of my life.

I didn't call my mother for Christmas or her birthday in the months before I turned forty. What little obligatory need I'd felt to call her on the other side of the country had flown out the window three years earlier when I'd given birth to my own children.

Instead of coming to meet her new grandchildren, she splurged on a trip to Ireland, the "homeland" as she liked to call it.

Admittedly, her decision to not come didn't upset me. I was probably dodging a bullet by not having to deal with her. Nonetheless, it felt like another slap in the face. That slap freed me from any sense of obligation toward her. From that point forward, it was up to her to reach out to me. I was more concerned with being a good mother than a good daughter to the woman who abandoned me some thirty-six years earlier.

The Christmas right before my fortieth birthday had been tainted, but I was determined to make a go at enjoying life and making it what I wanted it to be. I worked so hard and sacrificed over the years, sometimes working three jobs to put myself through college. Working sixty-plus hours after graduating first with a bachelor's and then a master's degree to ensure my success. Now I was also balancing motherhood with the daily demands of life.

Prior to my birthday, I procrastinated renewing my license, partly because, well, who wants to go to the DMV and spend hours waiting—especially during the holidays, and partly because I liked my driver's license picture and hated to give it up.

The DMV worker, a man of moderate build with a worn face, was probably pushing sixty. He called me up to the counter without much acknowledgment. "Next."

I walked up to the counter.

"Give me your old license," he droned.

I glanced at the picture of me, taken ten years earlier, and reluctantly handed it to him as if I were surrendering my youth.

He looked from my license to me, his eyes widening like he was suddenly noticing me for the first time. "What happened?" he blurted.

"Life," I replied, somewhat taken aback by his candor. But it was true. Life had sucker punched me, and that picture reflected the result.

The DMV worker looked back at the picture of who I used to be and handed it back. "We aren't supposed to do this, but I'm going to let you keep your expired license."

I stared at the photo of what used to be an attractive version of myself. "Thank you," I said.

I left with a new ID, and the old one was tucked into my purse as a memento of my youth.

So, my fortieth birthday came and went unremarkably. I received no calls from my family—including my mother—but I did get a few calls from a handful of friends. I delighted in my children, who were delighted it was my birthday.

2

It was January 2, 2011, the day after my birthday, and I received a call from my uncle, Larry. He, along with a few others, was supposed to come over for Christmas dinner but canceled that day, citing some stomach bug going around. He was also one of those who didn't call me on my birthday the day before.

I cut to the chase. "What's wrong?" I stated to break the heavy silence.

He responded with a nervous laugh. "Why does everyone think there's something wrong when I call?"

Another brief and uncomfortable silence followed. "Anne," he began hesitantly, "your mother was diagnosed with lung cancer a couple of weeks ago."

"What?" I replied, stunned.

"She had tightness in her chest and thought she might be having a heart attack so she drove herself to the hospital. They found out it was cancer. They don't know how far along it is and are sending her out for further tests and to start chemotherapy."

I knew this day would come but didn't expect it for another ten years or more.

"Your mother didn't want to tell you yet, but I think a child has a right to know," he said hesitantly. "I would appreciate if you don't tell her that I told you so she's not angry with me."

"Okay," I replied. "I won't say anything." I paused and stared out the dining room window, watching the palm fronds in the front yard sway in the gentle breeze. "I'll call her to wish her well for the birthday she just had, then she can tell me. But I won't say anything to her about the cancer."

I wasn't angry that my mother had opted to not tell me about her diagnosis. I understood why. She perceived me as a "foe" not a "friendly." That was the dynamic of our relationship from the moment I was born. I had come to terms with my mother's inability to accept that she had abandoned me. Because of her guilt, shame, and fear of how others would judge her for abandoning me, Marion never told people she had an adult child. The shame and guilt she perceived from her parents, her siblings, and everyone who crossed her path prevented her from acknowledging my existence in her life. Marion used the crutch of how becoming pregnant with me derailed her life. She was a promising artist who dropped out of college and married my father, who did not live up to her expectations of providing the lifestyle her successful father had.

As an adult, my grandmother and I developed a relationship that was more aligned to a parent-child relationship than a grandparent-grandchild relationship. I don't think Marion cared so much that I was closer to my grandmother than her. I believe it was that my grandmother was closer to me than to her that bothered her. So I was unfazed that my mother deliberately decided not to tell me about her illness and didn't want my uncle to tell me either. In fact, she only chose him to speak with about this.

Marion shared with him how she drove herself to the hospital a week prior to Christmas for chest pains. While she drove to the emergency room, she lit up not one, but two cigarettes while ignoring the tightness in her chest. When she got to the hospital, the doctors ran some tests and ultimately diagnosed her with lung cancer. The attending physician discharged her later that day and told her to follow up with an oncologist to start chemotherapy.

The problem was she had no insurance to cover it and no funds to pay it. She lost her source of income weeks earlier because she could no longer work. Fatigue and a lack of appetite over the past several months resulted in a massive weight loss. Hindsight is always 20/20, and it was now clear what had been going on.

I always expected one day she would become ill and need help. However, I did not expect it would be when she was only sixty-one and I was forty. Not while I worked a full-time job, maintained a house, and raised twin three-year-olds.

A little while after I talked to my uncle, I called my mom. "Hi, Mom," I said. "Happy birthday and Merry Christmas. Sorry for not calling sooner, but I was very busy with the girls."

She replied, "Happy birthday and Merry Christmas to you as well." Her tone of voice sounded part happy, part surprised, and part suspicious that I was calling her.

She mentioned nothing of the recent diagnosis and issues she was dealing with but certainly sounded down and out. I kept the conversation to a normal tone and length as though I called without knowing what I knew.

Two days later, my mother called me and told me the news. I let her tell me all she knew and listened to everything she said, this time truly concerned for her well-being. She had no money and none coming in. I told her I would send her money to help cover her rent and expenses while she applied for disability. The hospital had started her application for social security disability and state insurance.

My mother's calls started to come daily. They were mostly to vent, as there was no progress being made toward starting treatment because she had no insurance coverage.

A week or so later, on one of our-now routine calls, my mother told me at her most recent oncologist appointment, they decided she would be admitted to the hospital. She further informed me her oncologist had told her he wouldn't discharge her until she had the state insurance coverage to get the required treatment she needed out of the hospital. In the meantime, she would be able to receive the chemotherapy and diagnostic testing while in the hospital, as they could not deny her medical care while admitted.

I had to rely on Marion's report of accounts. She was hesitant to let me speak with the medical staff involved with her care. I had experience working in similar settings and understood how social services and medical care were predicated on applications for services such as disability and Medicaid, and I knew how easily it could be delayed for months. But I also knew how to keep the process moving. I pushed the issue with my mother to let me speak with the hospital staff on her behalf, and reluctantly she agreed.

Once she was admitted to the hospital in downtown Phoenix, I spoke with her assigned social worker to get her insurance, disability, and treatment approved. I also wanted to get an idea of her prognosis. Was her illness in the early stages that could respond well to treatment, or was it in the final stages where time was limited and treatment would be futile? *How would I manage this from the other side of the country? For how long?* Those questions stayed in the back of my head. I reminded myself the social worker assured that the doctors would know more in a couple of days, and in the meantime, Marion would get started on the chemotherapy regimen and diagnostic tests.

I made it a practice to call her daily on my lunch break. This time was also spent making necessary follow-up calls to agencies during their office hours. There was an old wooden picnic table where the sidewalk ended near the local dog park down the street from where I worked. I walked there, sat on the old wooden bench, and made the calls regarding my mother, her treatment, and the progress of her applications. I wanted to ensure they received what I sent the prior day and were processing it, as opposed to it collecting dust and falling to the bottom of the to-do pile. I knew all too well how someone in dire need of services can be stuck waiting and their application delayed because staff struggled to get through their inbox. So, I became a thorn in those people's sides that would motivate them to finalize the application and get it off their desk.

One afternoon, to my surprise, the hospital insurance worker actually picked up the phone. "Hello. This is Kate. How may I help you?" was her exasperated greeting.

"Hi, Kate," I responded. "This is Marion's daughter, Anne. How are you?"

"I'm fine, Anne." She answered distractedly. I could hear the shuffling of papers and closing of drawers. "How can I help you?"

"I was hoping you could tell me the status of my mother's application and what's needed, if anything, to finish processing it?"

"Anne, there aren't any changes at this time. We're still just waiting."

"Okay, then. When do you expect to hear something further?" I asked.

"It will probably be at least two to three days. I can't guarantee it, but that's my best guess."

"Okay, then. Thank you. I'll check back with you then. Have a great day." This wasn't the news I wanted to hear, but it was clear that waiting was my only option.

3

It was hard to pinpoint the date to leave to see her. As a working mother of toddlers, timing is everything, and time is precious and not something you have enough of to go around. I wanted to time it right so the days there had value in being effective in arranging my mother's health care needs, but I also worried if I waited too long, she might pass away before I went.

After several unreturned messages, I was finally able to get the social worker on the phone again. "Hi, Amy. This is Anne, Marion's daughter. I'm wondering if you have an update on my mother's illness?" I inquired.

"So, your mother's tests came back, and the doctor was able to identify the stage of her cancer." She paused for a moment and then continued. "She's stage four non-small cell lung cancer that has metastasized to her brain."

"Oh," I replied. I sat on the wooden bench, suddenly feeling deflated from the information shared.

Amy continued rattling off treatments and procedures and next steps that I barely processed. It was terminal, and although I couldn't get a firm answer how long my mother was expected to live, I finally cajoled or annoyed a response out of the social worker. "Your mother is all over this hospital, and most people on this floor aren't able to get around like her. I don't know how long she has, but it is most definite that when she dies, it will be from this cancer."

While Amy's response still left me with uncertainty as to a time frame, I gathered from that response and the online research about life expectancy and concluded she probably had a few months at best. It would be okay to wait to see her in a couple weeks, so I decided to go for two weeks in mid-January with my girls. I was doing my best to time the trip to coincide with her release from the hospital so that I would be able to establish services for her after her hospitalization, which would not be started until she was discharged.

My adorable three-year-old twin daughters, Emma and Catherine, had never been on an airplane. Despite spending a couple of weeks preparing them for the trip, the girls didn't do so well on the flight to Phoenix. We were all relieved when we landed at our destination.

From the airport, we went to the hotel to drop off our bags, and I drove to the hospital to see Marion. The nursing staff smiled at the girls and gave them tons of attention. They were to meet their grandmother for the first time. It seems my mother was responding well to the chemotherapy and she was all over the hospital, rarely staying in her room. As such, she was not in her room when we arrived.

I spent some time with the staff nurse trying to get an idea of how she was doing and when they thought she would be discharged. The application for the state's insurance needed finalizing. Once she was approved, she would be able to access all her treatment out of the hospital and return home. The holdup was with the hospital's social service staff, who were not responding to my calls over the past week to try to get this expedited quickly. Hopefully, showing up in person would help speed up the process. It was late in the day, so I would deal with that first thing in the morning, but for now the girls and I sat in Marion's room and waited for her to return from her ventures, which apparently she was known for. So, while my mother was on her deathbed, she was not on her literal deathbed.

Fortunately, we didn't have to wait too long for her to arrive, and she walked in wearing a hospital gown under a thick robe she had brought from home and a pair of white pleather sneakers. My mom appeared to be in good spirits. It was the first time I had seen her since her father's funeral five years earlier on her birthday. For some reason, they scheduled his service on her birthday. Apropos of who her family was.

My daughters, each holding one of my hands, looked up at her and I looked down at them and said, "This is your grandmother."

They both ran toward her, and each clutched one of her legs at her knees and they looked up at her face. "Hi, Grandma."

She looked down at them and seemed to enjoy the attention she was getting, not so much from my girls but from the staff and others around. "Hi, girls. How was your flight?"

They replied gleefully, "Fine, Grandma." Three years old or not, that flight was anything but "fine," but I was happy they were putting it behind them so quickly.

My mother went down to the cafeteria to get a strawberry-banana smoothie she discovered they made. She loudly slurped the last of it through the straw. I assessed her and felt a slight sense of relief. Amy's voice echoed in my head. "Your mother is all over the hospital." A slight smile and chuckle came over me.

I took in my mother's appearance. Her hair was longer than I remembered her wearing it in the seventies when that was the style. Somewhere in the muddled mix of the grays and whites was her natural hair color of light brown, which I had never seen before.

She had aged so much in the last five years. She appeared some twenty years older when only five had passed. I leaned over and gave her a quick kiss on the cheek and an awkward yet gentle hug.

She glanced at the empty smoothie she had tossed in the garbage can and asked, "Would you like to go get one? They're really good."

Having no other plans than to visit with her, I asked the girls, "Do you want to get a smoothie with Grandma?"

They responded exuberantly. "Yes, yes, yes! I want a smoothie, Mommy." They jumped up and down while each pulled on one of my arms as though I asked if they wanted to go to Disney World.

I looked at my mother and said, "Okay. Let's go get some smoothies."

We exited the cancer floor and walked past the nurse's station. My mother was holding hands with my daughters. A staff member asked, "Who do you have there, Marion?"

She replied, "These are my granddaughters. Say hello, girls."

They responded on cue with their usual enthusiasm, "Hi." They continued to walk toward the elevators a few steps behind me.

I peered back over my shoulder. My mother was enjoying being fussed over by my daughters and the attention she received from others because of them. I was happy to see the visit off to a good start and my girls enjoying themselves. *Perhaps they will have some fond memories of their grandmother when they grow older*, I thought to myself.

The social worker was quite right; my mother was all over the place, and I could understand the staff's annoyance in having to deal with her and me as well. It was a cancer unit in the hospital, and my mother was not as sick as the rest on the floor, not to mention I knew my mother's personality, and she was not going to be voted anyone's patient of the year. Although she might make the most memorable patient top contender's list. So, my mother, full of pent-up energy in her pajamas and robe, had wandered the hospital and found all the nooks and crannies worth knowing about. She discovered the cafeteria and a juice bar that made the strawberry- banana smoothies and a lovely atrium area in the middle of the hospital to sit outside. We continued toward the elevator. *Well, this isn't half bad so far.*

The elevator doors opened and it was a little more than half full, including a nurse asking those who got on what floor and subsequently pushing the button for each of them. We proceeded in with other people behind us. As the doors closed, my mother's anxiety was palpable and her eyes darted around quickly from person to person. The elevator glitched and shook slightly, then stopped without any evidence as to why or what cause.

"Is this thing going to plummet to the bottom?" My mother asked in a panicked and agitated tone.

The nurse quickly picked up on her anxiety and asked my mother, "Do you want to get off?" She pressed the door open button on the elevator panel.

Marion looked back at her and retorted, "Yes, yes. I do. Come on. Let's go." She pushed her way through the other people and off the elevator.

Phew, avoided catastrophe. She wasn't necessarily wrong about getting off anyways, and I was glad she didn't proceed into a verbal tirade on a packed elevator with my daughters holding each of her hands. I looked at my daughters reassuringly. *Hold on, girls. We're in for a bumpy ride.* I smiled and winked and blew each of them a kiss.

We took the next elevator down to the first floor and followed my mother as she navigated her way to the juice bar. We ordered three smoothies, one for her and two for my daughters and me to share. She showed me around, pointing out her favorite sections of food within the cafeteria, and then we headed to the atrium area, which was a peaceful retreat from the hospital, albeit in the midst of it. It was triangle-shaped with a lovely two-tiered planter that weaved around the open area with only a few white metal tables and chairs. There were two large automatic doors at opposite ends of the atrium, and the remainder was walled off several floors up but opened to the sky above. It was a lovely retreat for such a somber place.

Emma and Catherine ran around in circles, burning off the energy they had accumulated throughout the day. Several pigeons flew into the area, most likely seeking food from those who sought respite there or noshed on their meals. It was a good spot for a pigeon. As the pigeons flew to the ground, my children darted toward them, giggling at the chance of catching them. Now their running had a purpose—catch a pigeon. The game was on.

With the girls entertained, I sat with my mother and asked her about everything she needed to do so I could make a mental list of what to accomplish. Now I could help get her paperwork done for her insurance, so she could be discharged from the hospital and receive her chemotherapy and radiation treatment as an outpatient. That was my first and primary goal. In the meantime, I asked her if she needed anything, and she said she would like some things from her house. I made a list as the girls continually circled the pigeons, attempting to unsuccessfully corral them.

We finished the smoothies and we chatted, discussing what she wanted and superficially talking about what she was going through without any feelings associated with it. I don't know if she was uncomfortable, but I was.

The girls started winding down and losing interest in the pigeons, so I called them over to us. They immediately came to me and each took one of my hands. We headed back up to Mom's floor in the elevator, certain to avoid the elevator in question from earlier, and walked my mother to her room.

The shift was changing, and I felt it was time for the girls and me to leave for the evening. "Say goodnight to Grandma, girls," I said. They each hugged one of her legs at the knee again, and she gently patted them on their backs.

Her voice replied in a softer and higher pitch, as people so often do with little children, "Bye now." I watched, wondering what my children made of their grandmother.

When we arrived the next day, my mother was out getting a chemotherapy treatment. I took advantage of her absence and was able to track down the social worker, Amy, who was trapped in her closet of an office. She seemed to intentionally avoid me the prior day, but I was determined to see her today and tackle the paperwork that had stalled for my mother's health insurance.

Amy and I met briefly, and she was able to direct me to the hospital's administration department so that I could meet the staff who was responsible for processing her insurance application, which was essentially where the bottleneck had occurred. Emma and Catherine followed along quietly, as thankfully, I had let them burn off their energy first thing in the morning at a nearby playground.

We waited for the assigned staff to come out to meet with me. I had attempted to reach this woman by phone and had left her multiple voice messages over the past couple of weeks with not much success, but now she could not so easily avoid me. After about a half hour of waiting, she finally made her way to the front office to meet with me.

"Hello, Tammy. I'm Anne, Marion Sheetz's daughter, and these are my two children." I reached out, shook her hand, and continued. "Now that I'm here for a couple weeks, I wanted to stop by and see what was needed to finish processing her application so my mother can move forward with her treatment." I tried to not show the impatience in my voice and remain cordial, although I'm not sure I was successful.

"We still need some financial documentation to prove her lack of any source of income, and then it has to be reviewed by the manager for authorization," Tammy replied. She handed me a handful of forms for my mother to complete.

I shuffled through the forms, knowing I could complete these in a day, two at most. I glanced up at her and asked, "When these are all returned, how long will it take to review them and get a final decision? I know you can't say definitively, but just a ballpark estimate, how long?"

"Two to three days, maybe." She paused and added, "If everything needed is received. Don't hold me to that, though."

"I understand completely. Thank you so much for taking time from your busy to schedule to meet with me in person. I'll have these back to you in a day or two at the most. Have a great day." I reached out and shook her hand again, then turned to the girls and ushered them to the door.

I thought my mother would most likely be back in her room by now, so the girls and I took the elevator back up to her room. She was getting ready to head downstairs for her daily routine at the hospital. The girls ran to her, each latching onto a leg, saying in unison again with enthusiasm as three-year-olds do, "Grandma!"

She leaned down and patted them each gingerly on their backs, then took each one in each of her hands. "Do you girls want to get a smoothie?" she said to them in a grandma tone I had never heard from her.

They jumped in excitement and they both said enthusiastically loud, "Yes!" On the way out, I couldn't help but notice she was enjoying the attention she was getting from all the staff watching her interact with my daughters, but they were getting some attention from her, and I thought perhaps on some level they might recall these days when they were older, even if it was bits of what had taken place, and remember having a doting grandmother.

We rode the elevator down to the main floor again and headed to the juice bar in the cafeteria. "Three strawberry-banana smoothies, please," I said to the young cashier as I handed her a twenty-dollar bill.

After we collected the smoothies and all three of them had a straw in their mouth, we headed to the atrium area where we had been the prior afternoon. Emma and Catherine immediately picked up where they had left off with their game of catching pigeons after they deposited their smoothies on the table in front of me.

"Mom, I have all the paperwork that needs to be completed for your insurance to get approved," I said, and handed her the forms. "We can work on them today so we can get this finished tomorrow at the latest. It'll probably take a few days after we submit them before you get the approval."

"So I can get out of here in three to four days?" she said energetically.

"We'll see, Mom." I knew she was getting impatient with being there and wanted to get home, and I didn't blame her. "I would say at least three to four days, and be prepared for longer than that. These things take time," I finished, trying to temper her impatience.

I pulled out the list I had made the day before and started adding to it. I half-listened to my mother tell me about her chemo treatment and the details of her day. *She seems to be tolerating it well, at least for the moment.*

The conversation moved on to her hair. Marion's hair had been cut by the hospital staff to make a wig out of her natural hair. It was a free service offered by the hospital. "It's much lighter and easier now. I don't know why I didn't cut it sooner," she told me as she ran her hands repeatedly through her shortened bob cut.

"I like it, Mom. It's always been a good cut for you."

As we were discussing her hair, a staff member who worked in the small department for making wigs came out to the atrium.

"There you are," the young, energetic woman dressed in scrubs stated. "I've been looking for you all over. The nurse said I might find you down here. Your wig is ready to be picked up," she finished and she glanced at me with a smile.

I'm not quite certain how it happened, but before I knew it, I had agreed to go with the woman to pick up the wig while my mother stayed in the atrium watching my children play with the pigeons. I went along blindly without giving much thought to it, but as we neared the office, I panicked. *What have I done? I left my children with my mother unsupervised. She's a patient in a hospital, and I left them with her.* When the woman told me it would take a minute to find the wig, my internal panic escalated!

What if she left them there and walked away? The panic was taking hold. *Why would you leave your children with your mother?* I began to challenge myself. *How stupid of you!* I continued the internal berating and I thought of leaving and telling the woman I would come back later for it, but right then, she came out with the wig in a pink mesh bag. I quickly pulled forty dollars out of my purse and gave it to her, thanking her with a quick smile for doing this for my mother, all the while trying to get out of there as quickly as possible to return to my children.

The walk back seemed so much farther than it did getting there. I picked up my pace without turning it into a run, taking a few steps like a jog here and there. As I rounded the corner, I feared that my children wouldn't be there. I reached the sliding glass doors and they slid open. I took in the exact same scenario as when I had left some ten minutes earlier: My mother sitting at the table sipping on her smoothie while my children were running after pigeons. I let out a huge sigh of relief. My children were fine, and as far as I could tell, they had had no ill interactions with my mother while I was gone. I made a mental note to not leave my children anywhere with anyone. They would come with me wherever I went on that trip.

I handed my mother the wig and she pulled it out of the pink bag and held it up in front of her. I'm not sure what her take was on it, but I think the forty I donated would have been better spent toward a synthetic wig. I imagine she ultimately felt the same because when she later lost her hair, I never saw her wear that wig. Her hair was not the healthiest of hair, as she was not the healthiest of people, and it didn't make for a nice wig. My mother's cancer most certainly was a direct result of how she had not taken care of herself, and it reflected in this wig made of her hair. She stared at it for a minute, made some comment as she always did—my mother had an opinion for everything—and carelessly shoved it back in the bag. Maybe it was the confrontation of what her hair really looked like or that she would be facing losing her hair at some point, but she didn't seem to like what she saw and quickly put it away, both literally and figuratively.

My mother was beginning to feel the effects of the chemo and wanted to go lay down. We rode the elevator up to her room, obtained the keys from her to her place, and the girls and I parted ways with her, so she could rest and we could head out to tend to the tasks on the list.

Her phone rang a drum beat that had an ominous quality to it. She picked it up, looked at the number, and then placed the phone back down, letting the phone continue to beat the drums. "Bill collectors," she said to me.

Marion had somehow managed to buy a house prior to the market crashing a few years earlier. She most likely had obtained one of those no-qualifying loans that required refinancing a couple years later or having to pay unaffordable payments due to a high interest rate. A year earlier, she was about to be foreclosed on and subsequently was moving out of it, but not prior to the house mysteriously having a fire in it as she vacated the property. Subsequently, she received calls from bill collectors looking for money, and she had set the ringtone to the jungle drums beating, not unlike the sound of the drums when the natives had placed the woman on a sacrificial mound for King Kong to take as they summoned him to her. My mother's sense of humor was dry and sarcastic, and I had inherited that from her. I would've chosen the same ringtone if I were in the same situation. We both found humor in the horrors of our lives, and so my mother had set a ringtone of ominous jungle drums beating, summoning the horror to signal a bill collector calling her. I snickered at the irony.

4

It was a long drive to my mother's place in San Tan Valley from Phoenix, but the girls had fallen asleep, and I welcomed the time alone. I also enjoyed the contrast of the desert to the subtropical landscape I was used to in Florida.

I recalled the time my mother and I had dug up a saguaro cactus in a field some fifteen years earlier when I was in my mid-twenties. My mother wanted a saguaro cactus for her front yard, and so we set out to dig one up. We were placing the cacti in the vehicle when a police officer pulled up and informed us it was illegal and the cactus was federally protected. I didn't know, but my mother lived in the state for some time, and I suspected she did. The officer let me off. I was not a state resident, and he was inclined to let my mother off, but in the end, she couldn't contain herself. After she had mouthed off to him, he opted to charge her, and as a result, she ended up with a felony charge against her for digging up a cactus.

I spent the hour drive lost in thought, taking in the scenery and reflecting on my relationship with my mother. When I arrived at the exit for San Tan Valley, it seemed like a newer community being developed in the desert and was more affordable compared to other areas. My mother had rented a small three-bedroom house, basically a starter home, for the cost of a one-bedroom apartment in Phoenix. I took a few wrong turns after getting off the highway, but I eventually got my bearings and made it to the rental home. When I pulled in, the girls began to stir and wake from their nap as if on cue.

The girls woke with the pent-up energy of restrained puppies being held for too long. They darted out of the car, running full speed up the driveway to the door. I fiddled with the keys my mother had given me along with her list of things from her house and the store. I opened the door to a stench of rotten eggs emanating from inside as my children bolted in, each trying to outrace the other one with no specific goal of where to end. I yelled out behind them, "Careful. Do *not* touch anything."

Everything was filthy. I opened the refrigerator, mostly out of curiosity, to find it packed to the gills with condiments and other food. It seemed I was always cleaning my mother's fridge when I went there, but this time I simply stared at it all instead of diving into it. I then closed the door to allow the contents to remain hidden. The kitchen was tiny and dark, and the counters were completely covered with empty and half-empty wine bottles. I poured out the old wine that had been further fermenting on her counters down the sink, and a rush of sulfur assaulted my nostrils. I flinched and turned away. I had a vivid recollection of the days from my youth cleaning up the dozen or more beer cans my father would leave behind each weekend some twenty to thirty years earlier. I placed the bottles down as the recollection hit me like a ton of bricks.

I decided I wouldn't be cleaning up her place this time. I couldn't bring myself to do it. Instead, I turned to my children. They climbed on the chairs that were stained from spilled

God-only-knows-what, and I had them sit on what appeared to be the cleanest of the two. "Wait here while I get what Grandma needs, okay?" I put on a *Kung Fu Panda* video already in the DVD player.

I made my way down the hall into her room. The remainder of the house was as much of a mess as the living room and kitchen.

I walked into the master bedroom, and like the rest of the house, it was dark and musty. I subsequently opened the blinds so I could see. Marion had piles of clothes on her dresser and a mound on the floor that must have been the dirty clothes pile in lieu of a hamper. I grabbed a few shirts and a couple of pairs of pants for her, along with some bras, underwear, and socks. After taking in the dingy coloring of the undergarments, I decided to buy her a new pack of underwear from Walmart since I wasn't finding much in the way of clean ones.

My focus was disrupted by the loud dinging of the doorbell. It must be Rachel, who was scheduled to come by while I was here to pick up someone else's belongings. I placed a pile of clothes in a bag and dropped them on the table next to my children. I continued to the front door and opened it. "Hi. You must be Rachel. I'm Anne, Marion's daughter," I greeted her as I opened the door and moved to the side to let her in.

"Hello. Yes, I'm Rachel. Nice to meet you," she replied. I saw her flinch momentarily and squint her eyes as she adjusted to the change in air quality as she entered the house. I'll hand it to her, she covered her reaction well and quickly regained her composure, though she did appear to be holding her breath.

"I'm here to pick up an electric razor and toothbrush," she said.

I went into the bathroom, and she followed suit. I could only find a man's electric razor on the counter by the sink, and next to it was a Sonicare Waterpik. Figuring this was what she was here for, I placed both items in an empty plastic bag and gave it to her. She had a few other items to obtain, which I helped her gather, and she headed for the door.

She was in and out of the house in a couple of minutes, but once outside, she didn't seem in such a hurry. "I'm really sorry to hear about Marion. How is she doing?" she asked.

After a few minutes of small talk, Rachel left, and I returned inside the house to my children, who were still mesmerized by the cartoon and seemingly oblivious to the foul odor in the house. I took one look at all the cleaning that needed to be done and, feeling defeated, simply closed the sliding glass door in the back and all the blinds, returning the house to its previous state. I told the girls it was time to go, turned off the TV, grabbed the bags of my mom's belongings, and we headed out the door. I was glad I opted to get a hotel for us instead of staying here.

We drove to the nearest Walmart, and with list in hand and children in tow, we grabbed a shopping cart and meandered down the aisles, picking up things like deodorant, a new robe, pajamas, socks, new towels, and underwear in addition to the remainder of the list.

The next stop was back to the hospital. It was already mid-afternoon, so this would be our one visit for the day. I was a bit anxious to get there. We pulled in and went up to see my mother, who was not in her room. I placed the bags from our shopping trip and those from her house on the chair next to the hospital bed and then went out to the nursing station. The nurses smiled at my daughters, who were batting their eyes at them and smiling with a large grin on each of their cherub faces.

One of the nurses pulled out a bag of candy and looked at me for permission. I nodded my agreement and smiled. "Would you like something?" she asked in a high-pitched, sweet voice. Their eyes widened and they glanced at me.

"Go ahead," I said to them. They both eagerly reached in the bag and procured a couple of lollipops.

"What do you say?" I asked them.

"Thank you," they both replied in unison.

To which I added, "Thank you very much."

As the nurse put the bag away, I asked, "Do you know where my mother went?"

"I think she's having a test and should be back in about a half hour."

"Thank you." I smiled again, knowing they probably deserved it with having to care for my challenging mother.

I used the time to follow up on Marion's insurance application, so the girls and I went downstairs to the office and asked for the staff member who I had met with the day before. After a brief wait for her to arrive, I handed her every item she needed to finish my mother's application. After we went through the papers one by one, I thanked her and said, "Okay. I'll see you tomorrow to check on how things are coming along." She smiled a grimace that did not appear like satisfaction at the promise of my return the next day, but I wanted to ensure she knew I intended to check with her every day to move this along as quickly as possible.

"How would you like to get something to eat?" I asked the girls as we exited the insurance office.

"Let's go find Grandma first," one of them chirped.

The other one affirmed, "Yeah. Let's find Grandma first."

We returned to Marion's room and found her waiting for us. "The girls wanted to go with you to get something to eat," I said, and they ran to hug her.

"Good idea," Marion replied as she grabbed her purse. "I had a PET scan," she said, and we made our way downstairs to the cafeteria. "The doctor said he thinks it's stage four lung cancer and should be able to confirm after he gets the results."

This didn't surprise me much. I remembered what the social worker had said and all of my own research I had done.

We found our way to the cafeteria, and everyone picked something to eat. I paid, and my mother, with my daughters trailing beside her, found a table a bit out of the way for us to sit. As usual, I picked up a couple of things for the girls to split, and I would finish whatever they didn't eat.

"You're not eating anything," my mother said to me.

"I'm not hungry, Mom. I'll just finish whatever the girls don't eat." I had all but lost my appetite this past month.

I watched as my mother ate her food, shoveling it in faster than she could chew and swallow. She smacked something terrible and had condiments running down the side of her mouth. The noise of her eating grated on my nerves. Eating noises was my biggest pet peeve. Perhaps her loud eating was related to the residual slight facial paralysis she had from the brain surgery more than twenty years earlier or that she had been eating alone for years. But whatever the reason, it took all I could muster to be around her when she ate.

She looked over at me when she was finished and said, "You didn't eat a bite." She pointed to what remained of my children's food.

I replied, "I'm just not hungry right now." I took the trays and threw away what remained of our dinner.

Back in her room, I saw that Marion had unpacked the items I brought from her house and from Walmart while we were in the insurance office and was putting on the new robe I bought her. She commented on it as she stroked it with her hand. "I like the robe. It's so soft."

"I thought you could use a new one. Your old one seemed a little thin for the winter weather," I replied.

"Yes. It's perfect," she responded.

We walked to the patio of the atrium and sat outside. My mother continued to process her cancer diagnosis and tried to remain rational and not emotional. But the look in her eyes revealed that she seemed lost and distant, even as she continued on matter-of-factly. "Well, I guess that's that. I'll have to do chemotherapy and radiation in Phoenix. I guess I'll need to move closer to town. The social worker said I could get transportation through Medicaid in the meantime, but I'll probably need to come to Phoenix three times a week." She paused, reflected, and continued. "That's a long drive back and forth three times a week."

I continued the conversation about what her options were. "I was able to find all the paperwork for the insurance application at the house, Mom. We dropped it off and gave it directly to the person I've been working with instead of leaving it up front, so I know she has it. I told her I'd come by tomorrow to check on it." She nodded in acknowledgment.

I continued. "Rachel came by too, and I gave her the razor and Waterpik from your bathroom."

"Not my bathroom, right? That was my razor and Waterpik." She was starting to become a bit agitated.

"Sorry, Mom. I thought that was what I was supposed to give her. I'll buy new ones when you're discharged," I immediately added to prevent her from having one of her outbursts that she was prone to.

"No. Those were mine," she responded. She thought a moment and then continued. "Okay. We can stop at Walmart when I get out of jail here."

I looked at her face closely. I tried to understand why she needed the man's facial electric razor. I ran my fingers over my upper lip and chin, a little worried about the future of my own facial hair. It was not something I had contemplated before.

My internal thoughts continued as a realization came over me. It was surreal sitting there at a hospital on the other side of the country with my mother and daughters. This woman had abandoned me some thirty-six years earlier at the same age my children were now. I stared at my children, trying to figure out how she could have left me at that tender age.

It was getting dark out. A feeling of despair once again washed over me. I abruptly interrupted my mother's ramblings, and I called the girls to come to me. "It's time to go, girls." I looked at my mom and said, "Mom, I think I should get them back to the hotel for their nighttime routine."

Not giving her much choice, she followed suit and replied, "Yes, I should get back upstairs." We rode the elevator up with her and dropped her at her room, and then back down we went and drove through the city to the outskirts of town where our hotel was. The girls had a bath, and into bed they went. We read a few books until they fell asleep. I climbed into the shower and let the warm water cascade down me as I leaned against the wall and silently wept.

The next day was more of the same, and our Arizona routine was developing. Up for a hearty breakfast in time to take advantage of the extensive breakfast bar the hotel offered and then to a playground a few blocks away while I made calls related to services for my mother (her application for social security disability and getting her food stamps). The girls burned off energy and played for about an hour while I fielded calls and took down information and then called my mother to let her know we would be there shortly and to see if she needed anything.

When we arrived at the hospital, I found my mother was out getting another treatment. The girls and I headed to the administration office again and asked for the staff member handling my mother's insurance application. They called back for her but said, "She's not in at the moment."

I figured she was there and asked politely, "Please let her know I stopped by to check on the status of my mother's application and that I'll come back later."

We had some time until Marion would be out, and so we went to our "spot," the atrium, and I sat in thought, processing everything yet thinking of nothing while the girls resumed their running around.

My mother unexpectedly showed up after she finished her appointment, and we walked to the juice station in the cafeteria so all three could get a smoothie. I'm not sure who enjoyed the smoothies more, Marion or the girls, but all three sucked on the straws as my children discovered what a brain freeze was, each holding their hand to their forehead. They squinted their eyes as if that would help the pain go away faster, only to resume the process of sucking down the smoothie and experiencing the freeze again.

"I stopped by the insurance office while you were getting your chemo, but the woman wasn't in. We'll try again later," I told my mother.

"She probably was there and is just avoiding you," Marion stated.

I nodded in agreement. *My thoughts exactly.*

At this point, there wasn't much to do until it was approved. Once it was, she would be discharged to return home and then we could set up her appointments in the community. We chatted for a while once we were back out in the atrium, and then went to lunch at the cafeteria again. I once again watched in horror as she ate, wishing I had a pair of earplugs to block out the smacking noises that were so loud, they seemed to go straight to my soul. I tried to focus on feeding my daughters, and once again, I ate nothing due to my stomach turning at the noise and sight of my mother's eating habits. My mother looked at me as if she noticed I wasn't eating again but didn't say anything this time.

It was time for the girls to have a nap, so I parted ways with my mother, put the girls in the back of the car, and headed toward South Mountain, careening up the winding road heading toward the summit, admiring the scattered cacti along the way. The girls nodded off, mouths agape as their little heads flopped around while they slept. At the top, I sat and looked out at the city below. It wasn't the most stunning cityscape nor the most impressive of mountains, but I enjoyed the time to myself to sit in peace for a short period of time. I drove back down the mountain, and shortly after, the girls woke up. We found a park to walk around to allow them to burn off their energy again. Then we headed back to the hospital and once again to the insurance office, only to be told again that the staff member was not available. I said, "Thanks for your help, and see you in the morning. Have a great night."

My mother's doctor showed up a few minutes after we arrived back at my mother's room.

"I have the results back from your test, Marion," he said solemnly while leaning against the door to her room. "You have stage four lung cancer, and it has metastasized to the brain." He continued. "The treatment will be radiation to the brain, in addition to continuing chemotherapy."

As I examined my mother's facial expression, I could see the dismay in her eyes. She held her composure and was rather nonchalant about the diagnosis, asking the doctor pertinent and rational questions, but in her eyes, I could see the fear. I said nothing because there was nothing that I could say. It was what it was, and that was that. I would simply listen to whatever she wanted to talk about.

After the doctor left, she asked the girls, "Do you want to get a smoothie?"

They replied enthusiastically, "Yes!" So off we went and resumed the routine of smoothie, atrium, and dinner at the cafeteria.

My mother was a bit quieter this evening, but she chatted about what the doctor had told her and processed some of it on an intellectual level but without a drop of emotion. It was hard for me to stay present. Everything seemed absurd and surreal. I still was having difficulty even accepting that I was there and not at home in my daily routine of work by day and mommy by night.

It was starting to get dark, so the girls and I headed back to the hotel for a bath and the nighttime routine of reading books. After the girls were asleep, I stood in the shower and did nothing but let the water wash over me. I felt the water hit the top of my head and run down my face, and I stayed like that for what felt like an eternity.

5

The following day was more of the same without the success of speaking with the staff in the insurance department. My mom started processing more of what she was in store for and had her first radiation treatment that afternoon. It left her feeling tired, so we opted out of our afternoon visit while she slept, and the girls and I found ourselves at a state park out in the middle of nowhere, taking in our surroundings. It was desolate and isolated, and it looked like I felt inside—alone.

We went back to the hotel a little earlier that night after getting something to eat at a grocery store. We were all a bit exhausted at this point, and an early night was what was needed. All three of us were asleep a good hour earlier than our usual time.

The next day was more of the same, but we were a little more energetic from the good night of sleep. Breakfast at the hotel, playground to burn energy and make phone calls. I called the hospital insurance staff and left a message for the woman who avoided me the previous two days to let her know I would stop by in about an hour or two.

When we got to the hospital, we went directly to the administration office. I was determined to wait for the staff member today. I had given her some time to avoid me, but it was time to put a little pressure on her to get this done. There were things to do with my mother after she was discharged from the hospital before we went home the following week, and I needed her to finish this up so that I could stay somewhat on schedule to take care of everything else.

The person at the front desk picked up the phone and called the person in charge of my mother's case and, to my surprise, said she would be up in a few minutes.

After about fifteen minutes of waiting, the woman came out and said, "Marion's insurance has been approved and will be effective tomorrow."

"Thank you so much," I replied, a bit surprised it was finally approved and authentically appreciative.

She handed me a paper with information containing my mother's insurance as proof of coverage. "No problem," she said. "Take care."

I breathed a long exhale, and my shoulders dropped a bit at the realization that we were over this hurdle.

The girls and I went upstairs and found my mother in her room getting ready for her day.

"Guess what, Mom?" and before she could answer said, "Your insurance is approved. It'll be effective tomorrow." I handed her the paperwork, showing her the approval.

"Oh, great. I can go home," she said with a lilt in her voice.

"Yes, Mom. You can go home. I'll give a copy of this to the social worker, and they can plan a discharge for you."

Girls in hand, we went to the social worker's closet of an office down the corridor. I knocked, and the door swung open a crack, but not enough to enter; not that there was room in her office to go in even if she had opened the door more. I told her the news and handed her the form, asking for a copy.

She took it, looked at it, and then said, "Sure."

A few minutes later, I had a copy to give to my mother for her records. The social worker had said she would talk to the doctor about discharge and that it probably wouldn't be that day. I relayed the information to my mom, who appeared to be disappointed.

"Perhaps I should leave?" she said.

"Mom, I know you want to leave, but I think it would be wise to give it another day so that everything can be arranged, such as follow-up appointments, and give your doctor a chance to make sure everything is in order beforehand." She hesitantly agreed.

So, we continued our routine for the day, lunch in the cafeteria for them, none for me, smoothies for three, hours on the patio in the atrium, and, in between it all, a drive up South Mountain for a nap for the girls.

Waiting for discharge the next day wasn't easy. Marion's doctor had to release her, and he wouldn't be in until later in the day. Marion was getting antsy, and the mother I had known was surfacing. Her impatience was showing. The nurses had already completed all the paperwork and just needed the doctor to make his rounds.

Mom packed up her belongings and placed them on the side table and at the end of the bed. I suggested we go for a smoothie while we waited since we still had at least a few hours until the doctor would show. She agreed, and we went for one last time, three strawberry-banana smoothies. The girls sucked them down, stopping only to contend with the occasional brain freeze. We headed out on the patio, and I took some video of my girls running around chasing the pigeons. It was as if the pigeons knew this was their last day because they were in full force, darting about with the girls.

It was close to the time the nurses said the doctor would come, and my mother was getting more impatient. She was fearful we might miss him, so we took the elevator back to the cancer floor and waited in her room. I stared out the round, circular window and watched the sun disappear in the distance, looming large as it descended beneath the city beyond. My mother continued to become more and more anxious each passing minute.

"Maybe we should just leave," she said to me while staring intently at the clock as if trying to will the doctor there. He was overdue by about two hours.

"It's a hospital, Mom. These things happen. He'll show up, and you might not get something you need if you leave without him completing the discharge."

I felt her frustration and some of my own but encouraged her to wait and not create any other issues. The girls were getting restless, and I needed to tend to them soon or they were going to explode from boredom and the need to burn off their energy.

I went to the nurse's station and said, "Excuse me. Can you tell me how much longer it's going to be until the doctor arrives?"

The nurse replied, "The doctor is running late, but he should be here soon. Your mom will be discharged immediately after he arrives." I think she knew my mother was at her limit.

Another fifteen minutes passed, and the doctor finally arrived. He asked my mother some quick questions, went to the nurses' desks, completed some documentation, and the nurse came in with copies for my mother and instructions for follow-up appointments starting the next day.

It was now nine o'clock and past the girls' bedtime, but we were finally in the car, and to their credit, they maintained themselves fabulously. We still had a way to go because we needed to drive my mother out to San Tan Valley and then back to Phoenix to return to the hotel. That was going to be at least two hours, if not three, in the car. Luckily, Emma and Catherine were in good spirits and were singing and laughing in the back.

"Pull over here," my mother stated, pointing at a nearby gas station. "I want to get a soda and something to snack on."

I obliged her, and the girls continued to rattle away in the back. As I pulled into a parking spot in front of the store, my mother suddenly screamed at the top of her lungs at my daughters in the back. "Shut up!"

My heart sank. I wasn't surprised, but I was infuriated with her. This was the Marion I knew and grew up with. As soon as it came out, she hopped out of the car and proceeded into the store.

My daughters looked at me and said, "Who was Grandma yelling at, Mommy?"

Happy to hear they didn't realize it was meant for them, I replied, "No one, sweethearts. Grandma is tired and not feeling well from being in the hospital for so long."

They simply replied, "Okay," and resumed their singing and laughing in the back. I felt such remorse that my mother could not contain herself around my children. I had done as much as I could to protect them from her, but I hadn't seen that coming. I know for her it was the noise, and it was late, but they were three years old and had been couped up in the hospital all day. It broke my heart.

She exited the store with a bag of snacks and got back in the car. To my surprise, she said, "I'm sorry. They were just so loud."

I replied in a matter-of-fact tone, trying not to show my anger. "The girls didn't realize who you were yelling at. I know you're tired, but you can't yell at them."

She quietly acquiesced and said softly, "Okay." And that was the end of it.

Shortly after we got on the highway, the girls fell asleep. I glanced at them in the rearview mirror, and a slight smile came over me. They were so precious and innocent. We drove silently to my mother's house. She only occasionally broke the silence to provide me with directions of where to turn, which I appreciated, as it was now nighttime, and I had struggled to find it in the daylight the last time I drove there days earlier. We pulled into the driveway, and I dug her keys out of the purse, handed them to her, and retrieved her bags that were in the trunk of the car. I wasted no time saying good night, as the girls were still asleep, and I didn't want to leave them unattended.

"I'll call you in the morning, Mom. And I'll pick you up around eleven so that we can go to the food stamp office."

She replied solemnly, "All right."

After placing her bags inside the door, I headed out. I made a few wrong turns trying to get to the highway, but it was a peaceful yet long drive back into Phoenix to the hotel. Emma and Catherine slept the entire way, and fortunately I did not have much difficulty finding my way back once I was on the highway.

Once I arrived at the hotel, I gathered my purse and slung it over my arm, and with room key in hand, I scooped one daughter up over my left shoulder and then went to the other side of the car and scooped up the other over my right shoulder. When they were infants, I had learned how to manage to carry them both at the same time, which came in handy at the moment. They were getting a bit heavy for me, but I managed to get them into the hotel room without waking them up. It was around midnight now, and I was exhausted. As I drifted off to sleep, I felt despair at my mother yelling at my children. *How could she not control herself?*

I guess it was a question I had pondered my entire life.

We woke up late the following morning, all of us exhausted, but we quickly dressed to make it to the hotel's breakfast buffet before it closed. Part of it was already being dismantled, but we managed to get enough food to make it through the morning.

When we finished, I called my mother and told her we would be on our way soon. We drove back down the same highway we had been on not twelve hours earlier. When we arrived, she was ready and waiting.

As we drove along the Hunt Highway to the food stamp office, my mother started on one of her familiar rants.

"Those are chem clouds," Marion said, and she pointed toward the trail of clouds in the sky. "The chem clouds were created by military planes, and all that area around here is military installations." She pointed at the tall fencing we passed by. "The weather is being manipulated and controlled by the government, and they're running tests there in the Sonoran Desert." She pointed to different long clouds she spotted in the sky.

I nodded as I listened but said nothing. I found it amusing and also a bit concerning that my mother was a conspiracy theorist. But it wasn't really surprising that she had some paranoia. It fit who she was. I also knew enough that some of what she said could be true. I let her talk about it and educate me on the matter while we drove along the highway. I glanced back and saw Emma and Catherine leaning over in their seats trying to look at the clouds as my mother continued pointing to them. I imagined they saw butterflies and lollipops in what my mother saw conspiracy.

We continued along the highway and drove to the Arizona Department of Economic Security. I decided I was going to drop off my mother, who had all her required documents in hand,

and proceed to the ruins at Casa Grande that were just down the road.

"Mom, I'm going to drive the girls to the ruins and let them unwind some while you're in your appointment. You can call me when you're finished, and I'll come get you."

My children had been patient but needed some runaround time, and the ruins seemed like a good spot for them to do so. And boy, did they. The ruins were perfect, albeit it was simply a large adobe-like structure under a canopy to protect it from the weather, and then some small remains of some other structures nearby. The girls ran and ran around the ruins and had a blast.

After they had exerted enough energy, we went inside the visitor center, which was rather extensive, and looked at the displays before finding ourselves in the gift shop, where we each got a touristy T-shirt of the ruins.

My phone rang, and it was my mother. "Hi, Honey. I'm all done."

"Alright. We'll be there in less than ten minutes."

She got in the car and said, "They approved me for food stamps." She held up a debit card that was already activated.

"Well, that's great. You got your food stamps," I said as she buckled her seatbelt.

"No," she snapped back. "It's not great. I am *on* food stamps."

I tried to backpedal my comment. I understood what she must have been feeling. "I only meant it was great that it was taken care of and another task that needed to be done is completed. I know you're not happy about receiving food stamps."

She simply nodded her head slightly as she continued to stare out the window, looking intently at what I figured she thought were more chemtrails.

We arrived in Phoenix, and before we headed to her doctor's appointment, we stopped for lunch at one of her favorite Mexican restaurants so she could have an enchilada. I ate very little, as I was having difficulty building a tolerance to my mother's eating noises. My clothes were fitting loosely, and I was certain I had lost at least ten pounds these past couple of weeks.

We drove to the doctor's office, and I once again opted to drop her off and take the girls to a park we had passed on the way. It had a paved trail around a lake that we walked around until my mother called to be picked up.

Marion continued about the chemtrails on the way back to San Tan Valley and then segued into how she boycotted Walmart on Facebook.

"I have an account on Facebook against Walmart and their unfair practices. I hate to go there, and I wonder if they know it's me when I go, but it's so cheap."

"We can go someplace else if you want, Mom." I was not tied to Walmart, and truth be told, I really didn't like going there either.

"No. It's too cheap to not go," she replied.

So, we went to Walmart, and as we entered, she looked at the cameras in the domes in the ceiling up above her and said, "Do you think they know it's me?"

"No, Mom. I don't think they care," I reassured her.

We first dropped her prescriptions off and then shopped while we waited for them to be filled. We located a new electric razor and Sonicare Waterpik to replace what I had inadvertently given away. I was on the hook for these things and paid for them, along with all the other things she needed to get that day. Without any issue, her insurance covered the cost of her medication, and with a couple hundred dollars less in my account, we left Walmart and went to a local organic grocer, where she picked up a few bags of groceries, including a couple bottles of wine.

We drove back to the house, and I let her put away her groceries. I didn't know where anything went, and I wasn't going to be yelled at. After she put everything away, we drove around the corner to the playground area so the girls could run around some more, and then we called it quits for the day. The girls and I drove the hour drive back to Phoenix.

The next day, I drove with the girls to San Tan Valley again after breakfast and spent an hour at a nearby playground. I was getting tired, but we only had a few days left before heading home. My mother basically had everything she needed, and all had been accomplished and finalized the day before. She had an application out for social security disability, but there was nothing to be done now. I had the information for the office to follow up on that, but it would wait until the following week when I was back home in Florida.

When we were done at the playground, we went to my mother's house. As soon as I opened the door, I saw she wasn't in a great state. I could see the two bottles of wine that had been full the previous day were now empty, and she was hungover, probably a bit more than her usual state because of the interaction with the chemo and radiation.

"Hey, Mom. If you want to rest, we can take the day off." I could see it was not going to be a good day for her to be around the girls.

She said in a calm manner, "Yes. Let's do that."

"Okay. I'll call you later and see you tomorrow."

I quickly got the girls into the car and left. It was nice to have an afternoon off. We drove back into Phoenix and up South Mountain again, the girls falling asleep on the way. As I drove, I spotted a dust devil off the side of the road and marveled at how quickly it started and dissipated and moved in between. We went up the mountain, and while they slept, I sat looking out over the city again, enjoying the peace. After they woke up, we went back to the state park we visited a few days earlier and looked around the empty old stone buildings, taking in the western motif in the area. The day was a nice reprieve for us.

The following day, the routine continued again with breakfast, playground, an hour drive to pick up my mother, and an hour drive back to Phoenix for her radiation treatment. I took the girls to a nearby playground while we waited for her and then shopped for her and got supplies, an hour back to San Tan Valley and an hour back to Phoenix. However, we were now done with all the things my mother needed. We had one full day left, and I decided to take the girls to the zoo for the afternoon.

On our way, we passed the Desert Botanical Gardens. Marion said, "I've always wanted to go there."

"Okay. Let's go," I said.

I made a U-turn to head back to the gardens. They had several beautiful, green glass sculptures of giant, life-size cacti on display in front of the entrance. It was rather stunning. I had my camera with me and filmed as my mother had a tender moment with my children, and it is honestly probably the only one with them all together. She took each of their hands and guided them down a path and stopped and read the signs of what we were looking at, and for a moment I felt like they had a grandmother. I filmed the moment, knowing it would probably be the only time I could capture it for posterity's sake, but even more importantly for my own sake.

We walked further down along the trail, and I saw a mountain in the distance with some lovely Ocotillo cacti in the forefront that I wanted to capture. My mother, a photographer, watched me set up the shot and guided how to frame the cacti in the picture. She told me to do what I was already doing, but I paused and listened to her gingerly provide me with guidance in a maternal manner. I don't know that I had ever experienced that from her until that moment. I snapped the picture feeling somewhat solemn, but I wasn't quite sure why. I should have been happy to have my mother behave in a maternal manner, but it simply exacerbated that she had never been that way that I could recall in the forty years I had been alive. We finished walking along the gardens, and I stopped and took a picture of her with my daughters in each of her arms in front of the sculpted glass cacti at the entrance.

We went to the zoo from there and walked around, to the petting zoo and fed the goats, and then wound up taking a tram ride, since my mother had begun to tire from the day. We stopped for another bite of Mexican food and drove the hour back to San Tan Valley, dropping her at her house for the final time before we left the next day to return home to Florida.

The next morning, while we waited for our flight, we talked about what to expect, as we had done a few times previously over the past several days. I hoped they were ready for the plane ride back.

While I would like to say we had a perfect flight back, we did not, but it was certainly a significant improvement from the flight there. In the end, we all survived the flight, and I made a mental note that in the future, I will be sure to reach out to a mom who is struggling with their children on a flight to offer support.

6

My parents both had decent upbringings. There really is no excuse for their behavior and the choices they made, other than it was the late 60s and early 70s. It was a time of uprising and challenging authority, not unlike what the world is experiencing right now, some fifty years later. People were angry and at each other's throats.

What can I say about my parents, Marion and Clay? They were typical university students for the day and age. Both my parents were of average stature, with my mother being a few inches shorter than my father. They both dressed in hippie-style clothing, which was typical of the time period. Plenty of thick belts, bell-bottom pants and jeans, denim and more denim, and flowery shirts. Of course, the hair was long on both. My mother's hair was down beneath her shoulders to the middle of her back. My father's hair was long by his standards, with it down around his ears.

My mother's family was upper-middle class, originally from up north, and supplanted in the heart of South Florida in the early 1950s. My father was from a working-class family, originally from Mississippi, supplanted in the naval part of North

Florida. While both grew up in Florida, as did I, their experiences could not have been more different. Florida is representative of the country. The north and south parts of the state are equally representative of the north and south of the country, but oddly flipped. The further south one goes in Florida, the more northern the ideologies and way of life.

Albeit different people entirely, they did have some common ground. They both were the eldest of a large family. Marion was the oldest of five, and Clay the oldest of seven. She grew up in a stable upper-middle-class family in the suburbs of South Florida after the family moved from up north in her toddler years. Yankees displaced into the south. Perhaps that, in a nutshell, explains Marion. She felt displaced! A theme I think she carried with her throughout her entire life. Marion's father was a successful businessman who in later life became an executive in a well-known firm. Her mother dropped out of college after meeting and marrying him to carry out her marital obligations, tend to the home, and raise the kids.

Clay, on the other hand, had family that originated from the Deep South and landed in the naval area of North Florida, which was progressive by his familial lineage's standards but not by Marion's family. He was raised the opposite way of how Marion was raised. By his standards, he would have considered her upbringing opulent; meanwhile, for her, it was average. My father lived in a small three-bedroom house in which he shared a bedroom with three other brothers. His shared bedroom was two-thirds the size of the bedroom she had to herself. He found his respite from the cramped and chaotic house in sci-fi books, seeking solitude while she sought out attention and chaos. Perhaps they were both drawn toward what each other had and sought to escape their own life.

Originally, Clay aspired to become an air fighter pilot in the air force after graduating from high school. Despite the ongoing Vietnam War that most attempted to avoid, he dreamed of serving and finding glory in the sky. His dreams were diluted, though. He didn't pass the requisite eye exam and his application was rejected. Subsequently, he enrolled in school at the state's largest university, where he would later meet my mother.

Marion, meanwhile, sought accolades as an aspiring artist, having dabbled in music, art, and photography throughout her teen years. Marion even sang and played guitar in a folk-rock band in high school, and she aspired to continue to explore a career in arts.

There are only a few things I can recall that my parents had in common. One was terrible eyesight. Both wore thick glasses from the age of three, so I was told. My father wore the gold wire-rimmed glasses, and my mother opted for contacts. I lucked out in the eyesight realm. One would think I would be predestined for glasses too, but my eyesight was 20/20. One of the few things they had in common was that both their fathers had previously served in the navy, and subsequent family members had also been in the naval forces. Other common interests that brought them together were their love for *Star Trek*, The Beatles, and recreational drug use. It was the 60s, after all, and that is what university students of their generation were into. Recreational drug use paired with spring break led to my arrival in the world.

They married when they found out she was pregnant, and in early 1971, I came into this world. My father was an introvert, and my mother was an extrovert. She was loud and always busy. He studied business administration, hoping to emulate the success he saw in my mother's father while my mother majored in art. At least until she had me.

My father was happy to stay put in the house, while my mother was easily bored. Clay was in his own right feeling he had already achieved success. He had a wife and a child and his own place, which was already more than he had growing up. He was content where he was. Whereas my mother felt trapped and suffocated in less than what she had when she lived at home with her parents.

We lived in a small and unattractive student housing apartment that was a dive by her standards and all she had become accustomed to. Also, she found herself saddled with an infant she hadn't wanted nor had any interest in tending to. If she hadn't entered into a relationship that was doomed from the start and gotten pregnant, she would have finished her degree in art and pursued a career in her field of study, enjoying the bohemian lifestyle she had sought. This was the moment in her life she would never be able to move past.

As a child, I spent a lot of time at my father's parents' house and remember my grandfather mostly being in the back bedroom sleeping all the time. He rarely came out. He didn't eat dinner with us or much of anything else. He was either in the house in the back or at work. His existence and sole purpose was to work and sleep. He carried a stereotypical black metal lunch box rounded at the top that clipped over on the front side. My grandparents only had one car at the time, and they were always these secondhand, mammoth American-made vehicles. You could sit seven in the car, which was good because they had so many children.

By now, there were only three of their children remaining in the house, and then, of course, me the only grandchild. I always had to sit up front in the middle despite my grandmother being down to the last three of her seven children in the house. This was before the days of seat belts and children being restrained in the back in car seats. I was the smallest, so up front I went in between the driver and the passenger. Everyone else piled in the backseat, scrunched together. At times, someone might have to sit on a lap for the ride so we would all fit. That was always me, piled on the laps. There was no air conditioning either, so in the hot, muggy, sweltering summers of the deep south, the windows were always down, and my hair was always whipping me in the face. I think I spent most of my childhood with a rat's nest in the middle of the back of my head from my hair constantly blowing in the wind while riding in the car.

Marion, Clay, and I lived in the student family housing for a couple of years. It was a tiny two-bedroom apartment set up like a quadruplex but with multiple floors. I remember it quite well, as it was my stomping grounds. Clay would drink beer at night, sleep through his classes, and then drop them because he didn't attend enough. He wasn't performing to the level of Marion's expectations. Content with his routine, Clay simply enjoyed having his beer at night in his chair while he smoked a pack of cigarettes and watched *Star Trek*. I think, for him, it was a step up and probably felt like he had made something of himself. He went from living with six siblings in a three-bedroom house to a two-bedroom apartment not much smaller than his parent's house with his wife and one child.

Complacency set in with Clay, and uneasiness tugged at Marion's soul. They would fight constantly about anything and everything. Marion was trapped and saw no way out. All because of me. Had it not been for me, her life would have been a lot different, and I felt her resentment.

I was four when she left while Clay and I remained in the student housing. Marion rented a room in a small old house that was characteristic of the popular student housing area near the university. My mother would take me to student parties at night with loud heavy metal music blasting and beer flowing from the kegs. Blue Öyster Cult and Led Zeppelin were typical bands blaring from the stereo. I was always the only child at these parties, and I would wander around and observe everyone. I walked unsupervised as the young adults who were engaged in conversations glanced down at me quizzically. Occasionally, a woman would disengage from the conversation she was in to tell me how cute I was or ask me where my parents were. Of course, I had no clue where my mother was, although I knew she was there somewhere with a beer in one hand and a cigarette in another, engaged in some heated conversation with a guy. Sometimes, instead of a cigarette, it was a hand-rolled joint. I didn't know how they were different, only that the smell of the joint had an unusual odor to it. I was quite used to the smell of cigarettes, since I lived in a house filled with it pretty much all the time, but I didn't care for the smell of pot, and I am quite certain on several occasions, when the parties were held indoors instead of outside, I had a contact high from all the second-hand marijuana smoke I was exposed to.

On one such occasion when I was three years old, I was at my mother's house. My mother, as usual, was partying, and after a few hours of wandering around looking up at the people engaged in conversations, I went to bed. It was the middle of the night, but something woke me. It was quiet, not something I was used to hearing when I was staying with my mother, at least not at night. No one was there. I recall feeling scared and uncertain of what was happening. My head was swimming, trying to make sense of whether I was awake or asleep. I called out for my mother but heard nothing, absolutely nothing. I got up and went out to the living room and then the kitchen. It was dark, and no one was around. I kept walking back and forth throughout the house, which must have been no bigger than 300 square feet. She was nowhere to be found.

I went to the kitchen and pulled from the retro 1960s yellow dinette set the vinyl upholstered chair decorated with matching yellow daisies over to the front door. I crawled up on it and stretched to reach the lock on the top of the door. With some force, I was able to turn the lock, and the door flung inward, knocking the chair I was standing on. I thought perhaps my mother was sitting outside smoking and drinking, but she wasn't there. It was quite dark out, and I was so worried about my mother's whereabouts. I knew I had to try to find her.

My day care was a few blocks away and thought I knew the way there. I went back inside the house and grabbed my tiny orange- and black-striped tiger. I headed out into the night, a bit chilled by the cool air, and ran along the street barefoot, constantly looking all around. I had to find my mother and was feeling more and more panicked the further away from the house I walked. Passing by the houses, I saw no lights on, and all the cars were sitting in their spots with dew already forming on the windows. There was not a soul in sight, not a noise to be heard. I was so frightened, but I had to find my mother. What if something happened to her?

I became disoriented the further I went and had a hard time locating my day care. For some reason, I thought she might be there, or maybe it was the only place I could think of where to find her. I made a few wrong turns, but I eventually made my way. The building was completely dark. It was like going to an old town graveyard in the middle of the night, dead silent, still, and creepy.

At that moment, I knew my mother wasn't there, and I became even more afraid. *Where could she be? How would I find her?* This was a place I knew and was comfortable with, but at night it was nothing like that safe place, and I suddenly had a panicked feeling of vulnerability I hadn't felt before. I wanted to leave this place quickly and get far away as possible. A paralysis consumed me, and I couldn't move. I wanted someone to help me. I was utterly alone and afraid to cry out for help.

I turned to see how to leave to go back home, but I was confused. *Which way had I come from?* The hairs on my arms raised as goosebumps lined my arms and legs. I wasn't sure if it was from the chill in the late-night air or the fear. I needed to leave, and so I chose a direction to walk in. I don't recall which way I went, but I was able to make my way back.

As I neared the house, I could see the light was on and the car was back in the driveway. I was so relieved. My mother was home. I walked inside, and there was a momentary sensation of relief I felt that quickly turned to bewilderment. My mother was enraged and screamed at me. Without my seeing it coming, she hit me so hard and knocked me back. I clung tightly to my little tiger. She was so mad at me. She kept hitting and yelling at me for what seemed an eternity as I cowered to deflect the blows. I didn't know what I had done wrong.

When it was over, we slept in the same bed as we always did, but I stayed as far away from her as I could. The next morning, I sat at the old yellow dinette table, waiting for my father to pick me up. He couldn't come soon enough. The final insult my mother inflicted was when she turned to me and said, "I bought donuts last night. You could have had some, but since you left, we ate them all."

Aside from the neglect from my young parents and the occasional beating when my mother lost control of herself, all in all, my memories of my childhood were pleasant enough. I was quite gregarious and a take-charge child. I remember being the leader of my pack of offspring of the college-aged students living in student housing. We were unsupervised young children roaming freely throughout the housing. My big wheel and keen ability to ride it adeptly as anyone, even better than the boys, made me queen, or as I liked to think of myself, princess, of our little housing division among the big university setting. I told the other children I was a princess because I was born on the first of January. All New Year's babies were princesses, and queens were born on Christmas. This rationale must have worked because they seemed to believe it to some extent. I had asserted myself as the group's leader. The preschool princess! I would take them outside our little village area and explore the nearby woods, showing them where the river was, which was no more than a tiny creek. We would catch tadpoles and chase fireflies and butterflies. My favorite place, next to being on top of "the big hill" with my Big Wheel, was the playground. The seesaw, swings, sandbox, metal merry-go-round, and geo dome climber were all my kingdom.

That all came to an end at the age of four. My mother moved back home with me in tow, and I imagine it was her mother's idea. Marion had a part-time job and attended the local community college. My grandmother insisted she continue education and get a college degree to be successful in life. One day soon after, my grandmother heard my mother on the phone with her boyfriend, who remained in the college town where I was born, saying she had decided to give me to my father, which is what subsequently happened. After that, I only saw my grandmother a couple more times over the years. She never forgave my mother for leaving, and my mother never forgave me for being the cause of this fractured relationship.

So, my mother left. She dropped me with my father and drove away in the white Chevy pickup . I was supposed to have started kindergarten at the school my grandmother taught at, but instead, I was back at the university's student housing while my father finished up his studies, and I was enrolled in the public school there. And so started my life with my father.

7

I enrolled in kindergarten that August, but I didn't remain at that school long. My father finally graduated with his degree, and we briefly moved back to his parents' home. Boy, was it tight quarters. They had moved from the house my father grew up in, and although it was a new house on about two acres, it wasn't any bigger than the previous one. It was barely over a thousand square feet, with three bedrooms, two bathrooms, and a one-car carport on the side. One bathroom was inside my grandparents' room, so everyone else shared the only other bathroom. The living room was smaller than the size of a typical primary bedroom nowadays.

My father and I slept in the living room on the couch. Their teenage son, high-school-aged daughter, and their youngest daughter, who was five years older than me, took up the other two bedrooms. Boy, did their youngest daughter hate me, and, well, I guess I can't blame her, as I basically stole her thunder. She was no longer the baby. I was four at the time, and she was nine. I idolized her, and she wanted me gone from her life.

When I restarted kindergarten there, I found I was no longer the princess of the playground. The kids didn't really care for me, and I didn't fit in very well. Moving to a rural town from living in a progressive college town was quite a culture shock, even at the age of four. My posse was gone, and I missed them.

We stayed with my grandparents for a few months, and after my father found a job with a known company in a position that used his degree, we got a small place of our own. I could tell he wasn't happy. My father and I fell into a monotonous routine, the more so he fell into, and I went along for the ride. My father began to drink more heavily. He would drink at least a six-pack of beer and smoke about a pack of cigarettes at night while he sat and read sci-fi books and I watched whatever show was on one of our four channels on our thirteen-inch black-and-white television set.

Clay's excessive drinking meant I would often either miss school or be tardy because he couldn't wake up in the morning after drinking so much the night before. I was almost held back in second grade for excessive absences, and we struggled to make that "no more tardies for the remainder of the year" rule. I would shake him to try to wake him to get up and go to work and take me to school, but I was met with, "Five more minutes." After so many "five more minutes," I would give up and became quite good at *The Price Is Right*. It was a wonder how he kept his job. Although I was certain there were times he almost lost his job because suddenly the drinking would stop, he would get up on time, and I would make it to school regularly. But it was only a matter of time before the drinking pattern slowly increased, and soon he would be back to his chair with his beer.

School was challenging for me. While I was a good student, I struggled with fatigue because when my father was intoxicated, he wanted me to stay up all night and keep him company. He mostly spoke nonsense, and I often tried to sneak off to bed, but he would notice and start talking all over again.

I also was hungry. I rarely had breakfast since there was no food in the house, and it wasn't unusual for me to go without lunch, as my father would often spend the last of his money on another six-pack of beer and a pack of cigarettes.

My only respite was after school, when I would take the school bus to my grandmother's house. She would stuff me to the gills with heavy, southern meals. The ironic downside was that she gave me more food than I could eat, and the rule in that house was that you did not leave the table until you cleaned your plate. I would sometimes sit there for hours trying to finish it all. I can't fault her, though. I think she knew I wasn't eating at home, so she wanted to give me enough food for an entire day in one meal.

A couple of years after being left with my dad, I finally heard from and saw my mother again. She was still with the guy she left me for and was now married to him. Mitch was his name. They were living in an even smaller town called Perry. Even now, it's nothing more than a blip on the map. They had been in a horrendous car accident, and my mother was in a full-leg cast up to her hip. She had other injuries, but it's the cast I remember most. I was six at the time and went to visit and, on some level, to help, which is a theme that followed throughout my life. She would give me chores to do around the house. I also helped her stand up, giving her what little extra momentum a six-year-old could provide an adult. I knew she was hurt badly, though. Her spirit was not in her. She was subdued and almost nice. The fight seemed to have been knocked out of her.

I stayed with my mom for a couple of weeks and then resumed life as usual with my dad. We had to move from the two-bedroom apartment into a single-wide trailer next to a motel. It had a pool that people in the community could swim in for a small fee, but it was free to us, a big perk of living there. It was a nice-sized pool with a diving board at one end and a tall slide at the other. Prior to moving there, we would sometimes walk from our old place to swim at the pool, so it was nice to be living there now. It was the 70s, and it wasn't uncommon for us to walk places instead of using the car. My dad said it was because of the gas shortage and high prices, which may well have been true, but I knew when the car wasn't working well or when my dad needed that extra six-pack or couple packs of Marlboros.

Now that we lived there and I was a bit older, I went to the pool instead of being holed up inside all the time by myself. I still had plenty of that, but I was able to get out while he slept off his hangover. I became a bit more resourceful too. There was a small store that was down the path from the motel. I started hoarding empty soda bottles I found and looked in the furniture for loose change. Much to my joy, my father's chair was a good source of coins that would fall out of his pockets, especially if he had been heavily drinking the night before. I learned to dig in the furniture to get the loose change before he woke up and dug for it himself as it neared payday and there was less money in his bank account. Between the bottle recycling and the chair diving, I would come up with a good dollar or two, and when there was no food in the house, I would head down to the shack of a store at the end of the road while my father slept off his hangover.

The gas station had one tiny gas pump that looked like it was from the 1930s, and it quite possibly was with the large round orange circle on top of the pump that had in large print the number 76. The entire store must have been no bigger than a couple hundred square feet, and the shelves were so close together it was hard for me to maneuver between them without knocking something off. Outside by the screen door, there was an old vintage soda pop machine—the kind with a glass door that you open to pull the bottles out once you inserted your coins. It had the small-sized bottles, not the full-sized ones. I could usually afford a small Coke and a half-moon-shaped apple or cherry pie that was packaged in wax paper with the color corresponding to the fruit flavor inside. Green apple and cherry were my two favorites. It was about the least nutritious breakfast I could have, but it was quite tasty, especially when one is hungry and eating breakfast at lunchtime.

The same cycles continued. My father would drink, and I would make sure to go to bed at ten o'clock at the latest to get away from him before he became too inebriated. It didn't always work, and sometimes he would even wake me up out of a dead sleep to keep him company. The weekends were spent cleaning up his benders from the night before. I didn't like to clean, but I was bored and couldn't stand the smell coming from my father's corner. It reeked of a combination of cigarettes and stale beer. This was my life until I was twelve.

My escape from life during this time was the pool and my bicycle. I rode my bicycle every day when I was at my grandmother's house. It was freedom and escape. It provided me with peace on most days, but there were days when everything seemed so bleak and dismal, as if it would never end or get better. I started to have thoughts about riding my bike in front of oncoming traffic. There was a treacherous curve referred to as "deadman's curve" slightly outside of where I was supposed to ride. I rode there sometimes when I was having thoughts of hoping a car would take me out of this world. People drove so fast on the backcountry roads, and this curve was ninety degrees. Several people died there from taking it too fast. On days that everything was so dismal, I rode my bike in the middle of the oncoming traffic lane, hoping that a big truck would come barreling around the corner and take me out before I could even realize it.

Contact with my mother was limited to about twice a year while she was married to Mitch and lived out in Perry. I would see her for one week in the summer and one week over the holiday winter break. They lived in a little wooden house up on cinder blocks and both drove off-white Volkswagen Beetles. The cars were both beat-up badly and rusted in and out so much that both had holes in the floorboards with cardboard placed on top.

Despite having a second bedroom, whenever I visited, I slept on the couch in the living room except when it was wintertime and it was so cold in the house. During those visits, I would sleep on the floor on top of a few blankets at the foot of their bed in their room when it was cold. Like my father, they spent all their money on alcohol, cigarettes, and drugs in lieu of necessities. I guess that was something else my parents had in common.

Visits with my mother were always a challenge. I missed her and cried for her when I was with my father, but I hated the visits when I was with her. She chastised everything about me. I was too loud or too fat. Nothing I did was right. Listening to her was sort of like listening to my dad when he was really drunk. I wouldn't argue or engage. I would just wait until it was over. My goal was to be unnoticed, as being noticed brought me nothing but belittling from my parents.

The funny thing about growing up without much is that my mother and her husband, like my dad, all had jobs. While they may not have been filthy rich, they had a decent enough income and certainly enough to afford the basics of food, heat, and even a few gifts for birthdays or Christmas. But, like my father, they threw it all at self-indulgence on cigarettes, alcohol, and, in my mother's case, drugs.

My mother worked as a photographer for the local town paper, and her husband was a writer for them. I sometimes slept in the developing room while she prepared the pictures for the paper to go to print while Mitch was outside the darkroom at the typewriter, working on the stories that went along with the photos my mother developed. Whenever the weekly deadline approached, we were in the office for the night. They threw some blankets on the floor in the darkroom, and I slept there until they were finished. I certainly didn't mind being in the office. I was already sleeping on blankets on the floor in winter, and at least this was heated to a comfortable temperature. Food was a scarce item at Mom's and Mitch's house also, but when I returned, my grandmother would fill me back up with too much food.

So, the most contact I had with my mother was these twice a year weeklong visits, and this went on until I was around the age of nine, when my mother left Mitch and moved to Tallahassee. In a drug-fueled fight, Mitch became aggressive and was beating and even choking my mother. She subsequently decided to leave, and they divorced. I never saw or heard from Mitch again. He died at the age of fifty of a sudden heart attack, still living in the same house I had visited some decades earlier.

The next time I saw my mother was when I was ten. She was living in a house that at least had heat and a cot in the tiny spare room, so I now had a place to sleep at a properly maintained temperature. She lived not too far from the university, and had a stable job, although I couldn't tell you what it was that she did, but she worked regular day hours and was able to keep a job at this point. She still took me to parties, but I was old enough now to entertain myself with cards and sometimes would luck out and the house we were at might have a few decks, and I would spend hours making card houses out of them. I became adept at building three-and-four level houses and found it rather entertaining and enjoyable. When I grew tired of building houses with the cards, I would simply separate the decks out and play a few different versions of solitaire, and the time went by somewhat enjoyably for me.

One time, I was visiting my mother for the first time in over a year, and she took me to a New Year's Eve party. It was at someone's house that was a bit isolated and rural. The party spread out into the yard, and no other house was in sight. That was the nice thing about the northern part of Florida—your neighbors were not on top of you, and you had some privacy and distance from them. I wandered around outside and sat at a picnic table out back. You could see the stars and moon shining brightly beyond the tall pines that swung slightly in the wind.

It was closing in on midnight, and my mother was nowhere to be seen. The partygoers did the countdown and hugged and kissed, and I still couldn't find my mother. The song "All Over the World" belted from the radio as the first song of the new year. It was now 1981, and I was officially ten years old.

I was tired, bored, and wanted to go to sleep. And it was my birthday. It was almost twelve-thirty in the morning when my mother finally appeared. "Happy New Year," she said to me and then began talking to the others around me. About another ten minutes passed when she realized it was my birthday too, and she said, "Oh, yeah. Happy Birthday," to cover up the fact she had forgotten. "You know you were born at twelve thirty-five in the morning, so now it's your birthday." She then proceeded to tell those around us, and as they showed a small amount of interest and wished me happy birthday, she took advantage of the attention from the handful of well-wishers to turn it about her. She proceeded to enjoy the attention and tell me but directed to them about how I was born ten years earlier.

She explained, "I was two weeks late, and I missed my birthday by over twenty-four hours, and that was my grandmother's birthday as well. I spent New Year's Eve in labor, and then, although she was born at twelve thirty-five in the morning, we missed the tax credit for the year. She wasn't even the first baby of the year, but the second one. So, we didn't even get all the first baby-of-the-year presents." She enjoyed telling the story to others and having the attention on her. We stayed about an hour more and finally went back home.

8

As challenging as my younger years were, they prepared me for this next stage of my life. When I was twelve years old, my world began to unravel and spiral out of control. My barely existent relationship with my mother went to a new level of not existing. I was about a week shy of starting seventh grade when I went to see my mother, who was now living in New Jersey. This was the first time I had seen her in over two years, since she had married her third husband and would be the last time for more than five years.

Her latest husband was a professor of Asian descent, and apparently it was considered taboo for her to have been previously married and have other children, so I literally did not exist to her anymore. I'm not entirely sure why she even had me visit this time, as it was probably the worst visit. Perhaps she knew she wasn't going to see me for some time. After this visit, she no longer told people she had me as a daughter. She lied to people and omitted me from her life when she was asked about having children. She told me it was because of her husband's culture, but the reality is she had wanted to omit me from her life from the moment she found out she was pregnant with me. I was no longer her daughter.

She spent the entire visit chastising me, telling me what was wrong with me from the moment I stepped off the plane. I was too loud, I ate too much, I laughed too much, I weighed too much. I found myself walking on eggshells with her for the entire visit. Everything I did bothered her. My mere existence bothered her. Perhaps it eased her guilt to find so many things wrong with me, to dislike me. To turn me into something that was not worth feeling guilt over abandoning me. I was a lost cause, so what was the point? I suspect that she was trying to convince herself to ease the guilt of leaving for good, as she was about to do.

To add salt to the wound, a few days into the weeklong visit, I started my cycle for the first time. I didn't know what to do. No one had talked to me about getting my period. I knew what it was from my peers, but I had no clue what to do. I sat there and looked at my stained underwear and toilet paper and began to sob. I knew I didn't want to tell my mother. She surely would yell and lecture me some more. I would get the lecture I received when I was eight years old about how I would need to go on the pill before I was eighteen. I'm quite certain that comment was directed at how she wished she had been on the pill when she became pregnant with me. So, I stifled my tears and wiped the residue from my cheeks. I padded my underwear with toilet paper, went out to where my mother was, and sat quietly. I didn't want to risk what usually happened, which was Marion bombarding me with years' worth of parenting in one visit.

The remaining days passed like this, and I couldn't wait to go home. It was two days before I would leave when Marion came in the room and screamed at me.

"Why didn't you tell me you had your period? There's blood everywhere. It's all over your clothes and the sheets." Marion decided to wash the laundry and my stained clothes.

I said nothing as my heart sank further into my chest. I was so embarrassed, and I wanted to disappear. It was a rhetorical question, and she didn't care to hear the answer nor wait for one, so I was off the hook. She continued to berate me, and I tuned her out, retreating to my thoughts and wondering when this would end.

So, the trip ended, and like always, when it was over, I cried. I sat by myself silently on the plane ride home, looking out the window, tears streaming down my face. I was crying for the time spent with her and, at the same time, that I wouldn't see her anymore.

Shortly after that visit, she moved out of the states with her husband back to his home country on the other side of the world, and I didn't see my mother for five years. During those years, she probably called me a total of three times, and those conversations were simply her complaining about how difficult life was and how she was being mistreated and disliked living there. She didn't fit in, and the culture didn't accept her. I had grown used to not having her in my life, and I no longer cried for my mother at night to save me from my father's drunkenness. It no longer bothered me, as I was becoming numb to life.

It was around this time that my grandfather emerged from his cave in the back of the house. He started spending more time with us, and until then, it was really just my grandmother and me. They had one child left in the house, but she was in her final years of high school and was hardly ever around. My grandfather started to give me hugs when he saw me, and it seemed he was always coming out when I was there. My grandmother found it endearing when he would hug me, but what she didn't see was how his hands would run across my breasts, my butt, and between my thighs. His hugs were too tight and they lingered. I could not move, and I could not breathe. The pervert was fondling me, and not only did my grandmother not notice but it seemed the affection melted her heart.

Each time, I would wind up on the bathroom floor, sobbing as I promised myself I wouldn't allow him to do it to me again. I tried to avoid him, but he always seemed to find a way to trap me in a hug in front of my grandmother and slide his hands over my body without her noticing it. My muscles would lock up, and I would be frozen in place, unable to move or speak.

I spent more and more time riding my bike on the wrong side of the road, hoping as I went around deadman's curve someone would come speeding around and end my misery. It never happened. On occasion, someone would be close, but they swerved around me, and they would lay on their horn while yelling. This went on for a few years until I was in high school, and I no longer went to my grandmother's house after school. The years went on, and I became more adept at avoiding my grandfather getting close enough to touch or hug me, but sometimes he would catch me by surprise. I would simply cry in the bathroom, angry with myself for letting him get close enough.

We moved from the trailer to a condo when I was fourteen, which was closer to my high school and a couple of blocks from the beach. Although it was only twenty minutes from the town we were previously living in, it was slightly more urban and progressive. The older I became, the less time I spent at my grandmother's house, and I eventually stopped going there at all. It wasn't that I didn't want to see my grandmother. I would say she was the most important person in my life. But I didn't want to be to be exposed to my grandfather. I was done and chose to not go over anymore.

During this same time, my father drank even more excessively, and with that came new drunken behavior to deal with. It seemed I was shifting from dealing with my grandfather's attention to my father's. As they say, a chip off the old block or the apple doesn't fall far from the tree, so to speak.

He started regularly blasting the television in his drunken stupor. I ignored it until the national anthem played and the station either turned to a loud tone with a test pattern or simply turned off and the screen was filled with snow and amplified static. I went down the stairs to turn off the television, and he was passed out naked on the floor between the stairs and the television. I stepped over his naked body without disturbing him, clicked off the television as gently as possible and walked over his body to tiptoe back up the stairs. He was passed out cold and probably never would have stirred, but I didn't want to risk it.

This became our new routine. The days of him depriving me of sleep and demanding I sit and listen to his drunken droll were over. Instead, it was replaced with his naked body passed out cold on the floor. In the mornings, I would be cautious as I walked down the stairs, not knowing if he had made it to his room or was still passed out in the living room. One morning, I stepped on the thick cream-colored carpeting to feel something mushy like oatmeal under my foot. Wondering what I had stepped in, I moved my leg off to the side, and I looked down to see my footprint in a pile of vomit. Disgusted, I hopped on one foot to the kitchen, grabbed the roll of paper towels, hopped back into the downstairs bathroom, and cleaned in between my toes and all along the side of my foot. I then cleaned the smooshed vomit from the carpet, which was a disgusting task, and I struggled to avoid vomiting. This was to be a part of our new routine, and I had to make a mental note of how to evade it. On occasion, he urinated on the carpet in lieu of throwing up, which I found more challenging to avoid but less disgusting to step. On rare occasions, I had the treat of experiencing both in one day.

I wouldn't say Clay was a bad man, but he was not a good father. He was depressed. I do believe he did the best he could as a single father, but he was ill-equipped for the task. His drinking cycled daily, weekly, monthly, and quarterly. His other cycle appeared to be a gradual dissent each year, getting worse and worse. Someone once told me, "If you drop a frog in a pot of boiling water, he will jump out as quickly as he can. But if you put him in a pot of cool water and slowly bring it to a boil, the frog will sit there." That is sort of what life was like for me. I was slowly being brought to a boil over the years.

Things continued like this until I was sixteen. The only change was now that I was older, my father started not coming home some nights. The first few times, I worried throughout the night, wondering if he was alright. This usually occurred on a Friday night, but now he was doing it more often and during the week. Those nights were actually better for me since he wasn't home to harass me. I also had a job working at the local video store and loved it. It was the best job I could have imagined while in school. I was able to watch movies for free, and I talked to people about movies. I didn't make much money doing it, but it gave me enough to tend to my own needs, such as food and clothing, and on occasion I bought food for the house or paid some bills when the utility man showed up to shut off the water or the electricity.

I started to enjoy my life some. I no longer rode my bike into oncoming traffic. I had an escape from homelife and friends with whom I spent my free time at their houses. It was around this time the company my father worked at, for nearly ten years, closed down. He managed to make it to the middle of the pack for layoffs and received a decent severance package. As such, he did not immediately look for work and took some time off. For a while, he was happy and pleasant to be around, but typical for him, after a few months of starting to look for work, he became stressed out and depressed and began drinking heavily again. As he always did, he upped the ante, and the drinking became worse. I worked more hours to earn more money and worked most days after school and all day on Saturdays to contribute to the household income. It was the Deep South, and it was sacrilege to work on Sundays, so the store closed in observance. I usually spent Saturday nights with my friends, and Sunday tanning at the beach.

Unfortunately, my father's habit of keeping me up at night had come back. I tried to avoid him as best I could, but it didn't always work. He directed me to sit back down when I attempted to go to my room. Although I had never really been defiant against him, I started to lose my patience and say something smart back to his words of wisdom or impatiently say, "I have to do my homework." This triggered something in him, and he became aggressive toward me.

It first started with him grabbing me by the arm, shoving me hard against the wall, and getting in my face. It was so uncomfortable and hurt as he squeezed my arm as tightly as he could. He paused as he would do when drunk, but now he looked in my face intently and leaned closer as if he was going to kiss me. I turned my head quickly and pulled away from him, slipping under his arm and ran quickly to my bedroom and locked the door. He banged on the door and yelled for me to come out, but instead I went to my bedroom window and slipped out. I quickly went to my car and drove to the beach. I parked my car atop the sand dune entrance, put the seat back, and cried myself to sleep.

When I woke up, it was around six a.m. and I knew my father would be passed out by now. I drove back to the house and turned the headlights off before turning into the driveway so as not to alert him I was back, if he even realized I left. I didn't go in through the front door but snuck back in through my bedroom window and closed it as quietly as I could. Instead of going back to sleep, I finished up my homework then headed to school. And yet another new routine had evolved. One of me now avoiding my father's advances like my grandfather's, which I was not always successful at evading.

I don't know why, but one day he decided I couldn't go anywhere but school, work, and home for one month. Essentially, I was being grounded but I hadn't done anything to warrant it. His reason was I spent too much time away from the house and was never home, which was my intention, so now I could go nowhere for a month. During this month, his behaviors escalated, and I escaped to my bedroom when I could, slinking out my window, and sleeping in my car at the beach.

For the most part, I controlled my temper and didn't react, but simply waited it out and humored him to prevent his behavior from escalating. However, one evening, I failed at this. In my irritation with this unwarranted imposed restriction, I made the mistake of arguing back with my father. It was something simple, but I knew better. I was making spaghetti for dinner and chopping up a tomato with a chef's knife. He came into the kitchen to grab a beer from the dwindling case he bought earlier that day. He turned to watch me chop the tomato and proceeded to tell me I was doing it wrong. He started directing me to use a julienne cut instead of dicing it. He said, "You need to cut it like this," and he tried to grab the knife from my hand.

I blocked him as I continued to dice it and replied, "I know what I'm doing. I know how to chop up a tomato."

He screamed at me, "You listen to me when I tell you something," as he grabbed the knife from me and shoved me against the wall. He grabbed me by the neck, squeezing his fingernails into it, breaking the skin in a couple places, causing it to sting, and pointed the knife in my face. I said nothing and waited for him to stop. He let go of me, finished cutting the tomato, and said, "See." He threw the tomatoes in the pan, dropped the knife in the sink, grabbed his beer, and went back to his spot on the couch.

I finished cooking the dinner as I tried to make sense of what had happened, wiping the blood from my neck and feeling the sting as I dabbed the cuts. I made the two plates for us, and I handed him one instead of placing it on the table to avoid sitting next to him. I ate quickly, cleaned up the dishes, and went to my room, making certain to lock the door behind me.

It all got to me, and it began to show at school. After breaking down in front of my teacher, the school called the authorities to come out to the house. I was getting close to being seventeen and out of the house, but it was still so far away. The Department of Children and Families came to investigate and interviewed me at school about the incident. I was fearful of what to tell them. I wanted it all to stop, but there had been years of programming not to say anything to anyone, as it was a betrayal.

Shortly after the investigation, my grandmother called and asked me to come to the house but didn't say why. When I arrived, she told me the investigators came to her and asked what was going on. I couldn't say anything to her. She said, "You need to go get your stuff and come stay here." I turned and walked away. I couldn't go there. I couldn't spend the night with my grandfather in the house. I drove back toward home and stopped at a pay phone at a local convenience store, trying to find a place to stay for the night.

Then, to my surprise, my grandmother and father pulled into the parking lot. I don't know how they found me, but there they were. I hung up the phone as they walked toward me. My grandmother said, "Get in the car," as my father stood by. I moved away from the phone toward the side of the store and didn't say a word to her. She walked to the pay phone I was using and called the police. "I need to report a runaway teenager," she said. "Yes. My granddaughter. She's on drugs."

I had never used drugs in my life. I was in shock and felt the overwhelming need to escape. I backed up past the side of the store and ran. My father began to run after me. He stopped when my grandmother said, "Don't. Let her go." I ran as fast as I could. I ran and was gone.

I stayed the night out, and the next morning returned to the store to find my car still there. I got in it and went home. My father was there, and he asked me to sit in the living room. His eyes were bloodshot, but not from drinking this time.

"Sometimes I drink too much, and I don't remember what happened because of it," he said, and paused for a moment then continued. "Have I ever hurt you?"

I looked at him and didn't say a word. The silence was deafening and seemed to linger forever.

He didn't ask again but broke the silence. "We have to meet with the DCF staff, and they'll do a home visit and a psychological evaluation."

That's what happened next. At the home visit, I listened to a caseworker chastise me about how hard it is raising a teenager, and I had to endure the psychologist's hours of questions for the evaluation. I think we had another home visit with some more lecturing by the caseworker. On the plus side, a nice surprise out of the whole ordeal was that the house was as clean as I had ever seen it, and I was not the only one keeping it clean.

After that, I never spoke more than two words to my grandmother. If I answered the phone and it was her, I simply gave the phone to my father and went to my room.

It was my senior year in high school, and my mother had moved back to the states and was living in North Carolina. She called me now on a regular basis, knowing nothing of what had happened nor showing any interest or concern. She only called me to complain about life, specifically about headaches she was having. She would call and talk for an hour, not letting me get a word in. She rattled on about whatever was bothering her at the moment, and I became her release to vent. I was a captive audience.

Not surprisingly, my father had been getting back into the pattern of drinking and not coming home. I passed my time working as much as I could. I also made sure I stayed afloat at school. I had been accepted into a nearby university and had managed to maintain a high enough GPA to receive a few different scholarships. My final escape was coming soon.

With my father escalating again, it was once more becoming routine for me to spend the night in my car at the beach. It was a bit cold, but I stored a pillow and blanket in the trunk for those nights and would turn on the car and run the heater for a while when it got too cold. I would sleep for a few hours until it was late enough to where my father would have passed out and it would be safe for me to be in the house. On only one occasion do I recall he asked why I had locked my bedroom door and if I had left in my car. I simply ignored his question. How could he not know what was going on? How was it possible that after all those years of drinking so heavily, he had no clue what was going on when he was drunk? Yet, that's how he acted when the bender was over the next day. I was thankful I only had a short time to go.

Then one night, it went too far, and DCF was back again. I never returned to my father's house or saw him again other than a brief look as we crossed paths in the courthouse when I was placed in the custody of the state and became a ward of the court. I'd been told I wouldn't have to see him when I went to court, so I was taken aback when he was there. Fear set in me for that moment as he made eye contact with me with a look as if I had wounded him. He wounded us both, but as my mother could not accept responsibility for her choices, my father chose the same route of placing blame elsewhere. The DCF case worker, a different one than before, told me my father had been placed on suicide watch in the jail when they arrested him. I don't know why he would tell me this and for what purpose. I spoke with my mother a few times, and not once did she try to take custody or come and get me.

For the remainder of the school year, I lived with my boss and his wife, sleeping on their couch for the following several months until I graduated. Two days after graduation, I packed up my car and cat and left. I started college shortly afterward and never looked back.

9

I started college, struggling to get through and pay for it, but I was managing . . . barely. All the while I talked sporadically with my mother. She had moved to Kentucky and found a doctor who pinpointed the source of her headaches. She was diagnosed with a brain tumor at age forty. The brain tumor was in her middle ear, and surgery was required to remove it.

It was the beginning of the summer of 1990, and I needed to work to save up for college when the fall semester started, but instead I went to Kentucky to help my mother during her surgery. Her house was filthy. She was living in squalor. The amount of filth had resulted in an infestation of mice like I had never imagined. My grandmother, her mother, had also taken time from her schedule and flown in to help care for Marion. I spent the first few days before her surgery cleaning feverishly, scrubbing the kitchen and the bathrooms, even the walls and doors. I went through the refrigerator, which was packed to the gills and took hours to clean. At night, I was sleeping on the couch in the basement, and it sounded like a racetrack overhead with the mice running around in between the floorboards.

On the third day after arriving, we took my mother to the hospital for the surgery. It was successful, and my grandmother and I spent the time she was in the hospital continuing to clean up my mother's house. It was a disgusting task, but it needed to be done.

My mother remained in the ICU for a few days and then was placed on a regular unit for a few more days. All in all, she was in the hospital for a little over a week. She became more and more ornery as the days went on. I brought her things she liked or needed, but she complained and yelled at me and everyone around. Her face was partially paralyzed now because the surgeon had nicked a nerve. She couldn't move the left side of her face and had difficulty eating without food spilling out.

The surgery had also resulted in my mother's left ear being lifted so the surgeon could access the tumor, and she was left with staples that formed a half circle around her ear that needed to be cleaned and checked several times a day to prevent and ensure there was no infection. Once she was out of the hospital, my grandmother left that duty for me. My mother was highly agitated and constantly yelled and screamed at me for what reason I don't know other than it seemed in her nature. I'm sure she was feeling anxious and overwhelmed, and I was her punching bag. She unloaded on me whenever she felt frustrated or upset. I avoided my mother as much as I could, retreating to outside or down to the basement except for when her ear needed cleaning and rebandaging, cooking meals, and on the occasional errand my grandmother scheduled to get us out of the house for a break.

In all, we were there for about a month tending to my mother. At a breaking point, my grandmother tired of my mother's outbursts and abruptly booked us both return flights home scheduled for two days later. My flight was to return to South

Florida and hers was to return to Germany.

My mother regularly updated me on her progress. Her headaches were gone, the tumor was benign, and she worked at trying to regain use of her facial muscles. I returned to college a month later. I wasn't able to work much over the summer, having spent half of it caring for her, and found it difficult to save up enough money for the year, but with perseverance, I managed to get through school. I eventually graduated with a bachelor's degree, got a job in the area of my field, and prepared to start my master's degree program at the same university.

Periodically, during this time I would hear from my mother. She divorced her third husband and I never saw him again. She continued to move around the country, leaving Lexington for San Diego and then settling in Mesa, Arizona. I was twenty-four years old now and she was forty-five. I tried to look at our relationship through different eyes. I could see she was a troubled soul. She was stuck in her anger, resentment, and regret and would probably never move past it. She tried going back to college but dropped out before finishing her degree. She couldn't hold down a job and constantly switched career goals, which she was never able to sustain for a significant length of time. Usually, she couldn't progress as quickly as she would have liked, and she struggled to get along with others. I'm not quite sure how she survived and paid for things, but I imagine she received some sort of alimony. She never discussed it, and I never asked. In the back of my mind, I knew my mother would become financially destitute one day in her old age and probably need assistance when that time came.

She called me one day in an absolute tizz. She was upset that she had gone to the doctor for a checkup and the doctor offered to prescribe her lithium.

I thought, *Yep. I knew it. Bipolar.* Of course, I didn't say that to her, but it confirmed my long-held suspicion that a diagnosis of bipolar would agitate her further. There was some satisfaction in knowing my suspicions about my mom had been confirmed. If there was one thing Marion was really good at, it was denial. She lived there and did not like to leave. She asked me with an astonished tone, "Can you believe that?"

I simply replied, "Really?" with some forced inflection in my voice. "What did you say?"

She finished indignantly, "No, of course. I don't need lithium. That's a psychotic medication."

I didn't bother to correct her and tell her it was for mania, not psychosis. I also didn't push the issue. However, I received a slight validation that day that made it a bit easier to accept my mother for who she was.

10

I was in my mid-twenties now, and in attempting to have some sort of relationship with her, I visited Marion out in Arizona. I flew to Phoenix during the summer. My mom looked ten years older than her age. She had a Stetson hat on with a couple long, black and gray feathers sticking out if it, and she wore a pair of Teva sandals with matching tie-dyed cotton T-shirt and shorts. She had a pink-, purple-, and gray-striped woven purse slung over her shoulder, and the left side of her face was still paralyzed, so when she spoke or smiled, only the right side of her face moved. We claimed my bag and off to the Grand Canyon we went.

It was probably around eleven in the morning when we left the airport and headed out of Phoenix in my mother's beat-up old minivan. She had stashed a small Igloo cooler in between the two front captains' chairs and placed six beers in it with some ice. She popped open a beer, placed it in a koozie and then the cupholder, and she drove from the airport and onto the highway.

The speed limit was at least fifty-five throughout the entire drive, but she drove around forty-five for most of the extremely long drive to the canyon. She talked like nobody's business, and the more heated she became, the faster and louder her speech and the slower the speed she drove. When she really got into a subject that boiled her, I glanced at the speedometer and saw we were going as slow as thirty-five. I watched the road signs posted along the highway to see if there was a minimum speed limit. *Are we going to fall below thirty-five?*

It probably took us three times longer than it should have, but we finally arrived at the Grand Canyon. I saw some of its grandeur as she drove to the campsite where we would be spending the night. She brought along a tent and a few sleeping bags for us. It was getting late, after seven o'clock, and we needed to get the tent up before dark. We struggled but managed to get most of it up, which was good enough to sleep in for one night. We gingerly made our way into the tent, cautious not to get too close to the walls but far enough apart from each other. It was about ten now, and I was exhausted because I was still on Florida time, but excited to see the majestic views of the canyon.

I woke up early the next morning before the sun was up. The timing was perfect, as I really wanted to see the sunrise over the Grand Canyon and was concerned I would sleep too late. We had discussed it the night before, and at sunrise, I shook my mom's shoulder enough to wake her slightly. "Mom, it's time to see the sunrise."

She stirred slightly, and without opening an eye, said, "You go ahead and take the car. I'm too tired."

I didn't argue with her. The thought of experiencing the sun rising over the canyon in peace and quiet strongly appealed to me. I dug around and found the car keys and the map of the canyon to figure out where to see the sunrise. I found where I wanted to go and a place to park and walked over to the rim as the sun started to peek its head over the top of the canyon. The colors in the sky, the sun, and the canyon were spectacular, and it felt like I had been suspended in something heavenly. I marveled at the mixture of sediment in the rock that striped the canyon in shades of red, pink, and gray and how it changed as the sun rose higher in the sky. I took in its grandeur and enjoyed every moment of it. It was serene, and a sense of peace filled me again.

I tried to keep my focus on the peace I felt from the awe of what was in front of me, but with each moment my mind was on my mother and whether she was still asleep or awake waiting for me. I knew if my mother was awake for any length of time prior to when I arrived back, I would hear about it and it would set the tone for the day. So, despite my desire to stay put and sit for another hour looking out at the sun rising higher over the canyon, I succumbed and left out of fear, returning to our campsite, which was easy enough to spot with the partially erected tent. I returned to the tent and found my mother just waking up. *Phew. I dodged a bullet.*

We ate some fruit she brought for breakfast and drove to another rim and then to the Bright Angel trail. My mother's fixation for the day was water. She was harping on water, and she was in a mood, most likely hungover from all the beer she had consumed the previous day on the long drive. "People never have enough water. They don't understand how hot it is here, especially in the summer, and they never have enough water."

The more people we passed along the way as we went down the trail, the more irritated she became, and she yelled randomly at complete strangers who went by us. "You don't have enough water. You're going to die." The more people she passed without water in hand, the more she yelled and got louder each time. Almost like Chicken Little yelling, "The sky is falling." She felt it was her obligation to inform people who passed us about the importance of consuming water. As if no one knew and they would all perish if she didn't keep yelling this at them. She did this not only to people descending, passing us by going down the trail, but also to those ascending and leaving the trail.

We headed toward a slight arch on the trail and my foot slipped on some pebbles. I momentarily lost my balance but regained my composure. I simply slipped.

My mother freaked out and began screaming at me at the top of her lungs as bystanders stopped in their tracks and others stared with their mouths agape, turning their heads as they walked past. She screamed at me, "You could die out here. You have to be careful."

As my face turned red not from the heat but from utter embarrassment, I turned to her. She continued alternating between yelling at me for slipping and yelling at others for not bringing enough water. I said, as diplomatically as I could muster, "Mom, do you really want to do this trail? It doesn't seem like you really do." I paused for a moment and continued. "I came here to see you, not to do this trail or see the Grand Canyon. So, if you want to do something else, we can."

She hesitated for a slight moment and quickly replied, "Okay." Suddenly, she was no longer yelling at everyone, including me. Instead, we went to see the desert view watchtower and the historic village. We also went to the Kaibab National Forest and saw an IMAX movie about the Grand Canyon. We eventually headed back to the campsite and dismantled the tent before heading back to Mesa.

After another slow drive with my mother ranting and drinking beer, we finally arrived at her house. We walked into the ranch-style house typical of Arizona. Her house was filthy and the next day, I once again cleaned out her fridge and the kitchen. As I went through her fridge, she became agitated and screamed at me again. I yelled back, "Stop yelling at me. You don't always have to scream at me!" This did nothing but agitate her more, and she escalated and screamed on. About what, I don't even remember. But I had had enough, and I told her so.

I suddenly found myself mimicking my mother, screaming at her, "That's it! I can't take it anymore! All you do is yell and scream and complain about everything!" I turned to grab my bag and continued. "I'm leaving. I can't take anymore of this from you! All you ever do is scream at me. My whole life all you've ever done is yell at me, chastise me, and criticize me."

To my amazement, my mother suddenly broke down crying, sobbing like I had never seen her cry, and for some reason, it broke my heart. I reached out, grabbed her, and hugged her for a moment as I clinched my teeth, folded my lips inward, and held back my own tears.

While I hugged her, she said, "Please don't tell my mother I'm a bad mother. Please don't tell them I'm a bad mother."

I let her go, and she wiped the tears from her face. I looked at her and paused for a moment, reflecting on what she said, and responded without malice, anger, or dismay that she once again only thought of herself. "Okay, Mom. I won't say anything bad about you." She didn't regret what she did to me, only the consequences in her family relationships it caused her. Perhaps if she could get past that, we could have some sort of relationship. Once she became pregnant with me, she was damned no matter what choice she made. Even though I understood where she was coming from, I also knew I was done and decided to leave the next day.

11

I was now thirty-four years old, long finished with my degrees, and working a full-time job. Over the years, I periodically heard from my mother and learned to tolerate her calls. There were times I even called to check up on her if I hadn't heard from her for some time. I compartmentalized it all and put it away. My mother would never change, and my childhood was long gone and a distant memory. This is who my mother was, and I was resigned to it. In the back of my mind, I knew I would need to prepare to take care of my mother in her older days, most likely when I was in my late fifties or later, but for now, it was what it was.

My relationship with her continued to be occasional phone conversations a few times a year. Sometimes I talked to her on the holidays and sometimes not. It depended on if I felt I could tolerate the conversation. If I couldn't handle it, I didn't call her and let her calls go to voicemail, not returning the call until I felt up for it. The invention of caller ID was fantastic and made it easy to decide.

The next time I saw her was roughly ten years later when I went to Arizona to visit. Her father, my grandfather, now lived in Key Biscayne, about an hour away from me, although I never saw or heard from him. He was getting older, as was she, so she decided to visit him because she worried she wouldn't see him again.

"He's getting really old, and I want to see him one last time before he dies," she said.

I had been working at a new job for about six months and was hesitant to take a day off from work, but ultimately, I decided to take the day and spend it with her.

We had a decent enough visit that was significantly helped by the rum and cokes I drank at the cabana bar down by the pool off the beach in South Miami. We had dinner at the country club to which my grandfather was a member. He picked us up at the hotel and then dropped us off right after eating, which, all in all, took less than two hours. This was what he was doing with her daily. Their visits consisted of nothing more than having dinner each evening while she stayed alone in the upscale hotel in a coveted vacation spot in Miami. Somehow, it saddened me how alone she was.

She was right about visiting him then, about seeing him again before he died. That would be the last time she, or I for that matter, would see him alive. A little over six months later, on the day after Christmas in the parking lot right next to the car after having lunch at that very country club, he succumbed to a sudden heart attack. My mother flew into town for the funeral, which happened to be on her fifty-sixth birthday.

I felt that was very telling of her family that they planned his funeral on her birthday. What a cruel thing to do to her, to anyone. It's hard to believe that was not done deliberately. Ironically, after the funeral, I spoke with my grandfather's wife, who I had not seen in some twenty years or so. She had been unaware that my grandfather had seen my mother earlier that year or even that my grandfather had arranged for my mother to visit him. That one dinner with my mother and grandfather is the only memory I have of being with the two of them together at the same time.

12

It was February 2011, and my mother had been in treatment for a few weeks. In all, it was a calm month. The visit with the girls had been rather successful, and at the time, my mother and I were probably getting along the best in our entire lives.

I was back home and established a new routine. Monday through Friday was quite rote. Get up at six a.m., make my coffee, let the dog out and possibly a cat or two as well. Take a quick shower, get dressed, and then make breakfast. Time to wake the girls and feed them while making their lunches. Drop the girls at their day care, which was a block behind the house. Off to work I went. I walked for fifteen to twenty minutes, morning and afternoon, during my breaks and then for an hour at lunchtime. I used the time to call and follow up on my mother's needs, such as her application for long-term care and her social security disability application. I then called my mom to check on her and see how she was doing and update her with the status of her applications. Afternoons after work and weekends were for the girls. Things were smoothing out a bit and seemed manageable.

March rolled around, and my mother was making progress with her treatment. All the online searching I had done indicated the level of her illness should have resulted in her death within a few months of her diagnosis. Ironically, people would tell me of how someone they knew had been diagnosed with stage four lung cancer also, and they were gone within weeks of the diagnosis. Somehow my mother managed not only to stay alive but she seemed to be getting better. She told me her tumors shrank and that hospice services stopped due to her improved health. They would continue when needed, but she no longer met their requirements for services anymore.

This was confirmed by the nurse I had been dealing with to arrange long-term care placement for her when the time came and she could no longer live independently. After the paperwork was completed and she met the qualifying financial criteria, she met the nursing assessment criteria for care. The nurse called and informed me she no longer met the physical requirements for long-term care due to her progress as a result of her treatment. She responded very well to the radiation and chemotherapy—to the point the tumors were almost negligible. I was beginning to think my mother's concoction she discovered for Essiac tea may actually be truly curing her cancer as she said it was.

The nurse further advised that because of the length of time it took to go through the entire application process, she was going to leave it open, and when the time came, and my mother began to decline in health, they would reevaluate her from a nursing perspective to approve her application. She made it very clear and said not to reapply with a new application. Doing a new application would result in the current one being closed, and it would restart the entire process, most likely not getting approved in time for her to receive services prior to her passing away. I thanked her for her help and felt such relief at having such a good nurse to work with on this issue. The long-term care services were going to be so valuable when the time came. She could possibly remain in her place with nursing staff coming in to tend to her, or if needed, a bed would be provided in a facility with full-time staffing. Couple that with the hospice services she would be able to receive, and again I felt relieved about her needs being met when the time came.

Essiac tea was my mother's obsession now. She believed she could beat the cancer, and I was beginning to think it might be possible too. Afterall, she should have been dead by now or certainly closer to it. So, my mother bought her Essiac tea powder in bulk form, and making her tea became her religion.

The process of making her tea was an arduous one. Her recipe called for two ounces of herbs added to five quarts of boiling water that simmered on the stove for hours on end. She would stir it every two hours over twelve hours and then reheat it to a boil. The next step required a strainer with cheesecloth placed over it, which she used to transfer the tea to another bowl in order to remove the sediment from the liquid. Then she used a funnel to pour it into an old plastic water jug. It was then placed in the refrigerator to cool until consumption. The recipe called for precision, and she attended to each step in the recipe.

She then would consume a cup every four hours. She was so fanatical about it that she would set an alarm to wake up in the middle of the night to consume it or to stir the tea if she was in the midst of making it. During phone calls, her alarm would go off and she would go tend to her Essiac tea while it was boiling. Mom would make her tea two to three times a week. Her days were becoming full and even more fulfilling for her. She had some mild response and occasional bouts of nausea, but for the most part, she was coping well with the treatment.

In April, she moved from San Tan Valley into a one-bedroom apartment in downtown Phoenix so that she was closer to her treatment and doctors' offices. Instead of the hour ride there and back, she could drive there and back in fifteen minutes. It also placed her closer to places, such as the Arizona Mills mall. She started going there every day and walking around inside to keep up her strength and stamina. She would walk anywhere from thirty minutes to an hour each day.

She was content from what I could tell, which is probably the only time in my life I would have described her with that word. I was still sending her some spending money, so she had some extra to enjoy herself. She was getting some help from her ex-husband and her disability. For the first time in her life, I would say she was thriving.

In May, my mother told me she was continuing with her treatment and that there was no change. She seemed a little out of it at times, but she assured me she was fine. She didn't want me calling her doctors, and given her history of paranoia and the confirmation I had received elsewhere regarding her current well-being, I left well enough alone.

13

It was now the beginning of June, and I found out that what I believed to be true about the continued progress of my mother's health was not. In one eventful day, I learned my growing optimism was built on a faulty foundation, and that foundation sunk. Marion was no longer progressing and doing well; she, in fact, stopped her treatment, and her tumors were growing significantly. She told me the same story for the past several weeks, but in reality, her tumors stopped responding to the treatment, and the doctor ceased her treatment and referred her back to hospice. I was once again sucker-punched. The rug was pulled out from under me.

I tried to piece the puzzle back together, but nothing was quite fitting. "Mom, what do you mean you're no longer getting radiation?" I asked her after she replied to my routine question of how her appointment was.

"I stopped a few weeks ago," she said as if I were late to the party.

"You stopped a few weeks ago?" I pressed on despite her annoyance.

"Yes," she snapped back.

Knowing how my mother would escalate quickly, I paused and moderated my voice, speaking with intent to diffuse her somewhat. "Mom, I don't remember and thought you were still getting your treatment. So, what you're saying is you haven't had it in a few weeks now? Any of it? The radiation and the chemo?"

She responded with a simple but not so argumentative, "Yes." She offered nothing further, though.

"Why did you stop the treatment, Mom?" I pressed further.

"The doctor stopped it a few weeks ago," she retorted.

I could tell I was getting nowhere with this, and something inside said it wasn't her usual personality of obfuscating deliberately that was going on. "Mom, I want to call your doctor to hear from him what's going on. I know you don't like for me to, but I want you to let me speak with the staff, okay?"

I prepared for her to become angry with me and start the usual paranoia that I was out to get her and interfere with her, but to my surprise, she simply responded, "Okay."

The next day on my lunch break, I sat at the same outdoor table as always and placed the call to my mother's oncologist. I really didn't know what to expect from them. I figured she wouldn't have listed me as a contact to release information to, and I was half expecting them to tell me, "Sorry, we can't give you that information without a release from the patient." My mother would yes me to death but never do it. Her paranoia being what it was, I would expect no less.

I was placed on hold to speak with the nurse, and I don't know if the nurse even bothered to look if there was a release from my mother or not, but after providing some of her basic information such as phone, address, and date of birth, I was in. The nurse told me my mother's tumors had stopped responding to the treatment about a month prior, and as such, the treatment was discontinued and she was referred back to hospice. Because she was back with hospice, there would be no further treatment for the cancer other than to make her comfortable.

I realized that my mother was not necessarily deliberately omitting information when talking to me but that she was having difficulties remembering because of the cancer and possibly the treatment too. At that moment, I felt like I had failed. I was not vigilant enough and should have known better than to rely on obtaining all my information from her. I should have insisted that she let me follow up with her doctor's office.

I accessed my phone book and called the admission coordinator nurse with the long-term care department of Arizona and left a message letting her know my mother's health had declined and asked what was needed in order to continue my mother's application and get another medical necessity evaluation.

The following day, the routine was the same as the one before, only this time I called the Hospice of the Valley and left a message. The week continued to play out the same, often resulting in phone tag until I connected with people. I resumed the routine of daily calls at lunchtime to attend to my mother's services to prepare for the inevitable.

Calls with her now were becoming a bit confusing. Some days what she told me seemed to conflict with what the previous day's conversation yielded. What was going on with her? I began to wonder if we were heading for that quick dissent and rapid deterioration in her health that I had anticipated six months earlier. Were we there now? I needed to get things in order for her end-of-life plan. People fail to realize that if you don't arrange these services in advance, they won't be there until after you need them. In this case, they won't be available until after she is dead. What's the point of that?

I knew enough to plan ahead, and we were ahead of the game on that. I couldn't rely on my mother for accurate information, and I would need to go to other sources to communicate directly with them or this would fail. That was a tricky predicament to be in. Oddly enough, she was the one who abandoned me, and it was me who was at risk of being shut out completely. She would be sunk if she did this. I knew that. She had shut out so many other people from her life, perhaps because of me, because of her choices regarding me, and how they viewed her because of it. I couldn't give her friendship or open myself up to her, but I could be sure she had what she needed to ensure she was comfortable and her basic needs were taken care of while she was in her final days. I could do that.

It was midway through the month now and I had finally reached her hospice workers. She had a nurse and two social workers or counselors assigned, and they were doing her readmission assessments. It was time to go back out to see her. This time, I would go without my daughters. It would be the first time I wouldn't see them for an extended period and spend a night away from them. I hated to leave, but I couldn't take them with me for this. I couldn't trust my mother around them. She was starting to display her true nature that I remembered from being a young child. She was angry and prone to outbursts, yelling and screaming and causing a scene. Out of control and unpredictable. I would not allow my children to be around that.

I made arrangements to fly out the next week and planned to stay for ten days. Although it didn't sound like the end was imminent, it was certainly closing in on me and her. I wanted to make sure she had everything she needed until such time she needed additional help. I also needed to figure out what was in place and what still needed to be done, and there were limitations on being able to do this from the other side of the country.

I spent the next couple of days arranging a meeting with hospice staff at my mom's apartment. I finally spoke with the admissions nurse for long-term care, and she told me to continue the process of evaluating my mother again from a medical standpoint so that she would be accepted for services. She strongly reiterated that a new application could not be submitted. If it was, it would result in the current application being closed and would delay her receiving services because they would have to once again determine financial eligibility, which would take at least a couple of months again prior to assessing her medically to determine her final eligibility. She felt confident that my mom was now at the level that she would qualify for long-term care services, which would give her in-home care and then placement in a facility if and when the time came that she needed 24-hour care. I was so thankful for this woman and the services they would provide my mother. I gave her the information on my mother's hospice services and thanked her repeatedly for all her help.

As I prepared for my trip, I told my daughters that I was going to take a plane to see Grandma again to take care of her. I hated to leave them for such a long time and be so far away from them. But in the back of my mind, I told myself I was doing the right thing. My mother needed someone to do this for her, and people should have others who help them in their time of need. In their time of death.

14

July 2011

I don't recall much about the flight or getting there. It was certainly uneventful compared to the previous flight six months earlier with my two little ones. It took some time to get through the line and obtain the rental car, head to the hotel to drop by bags, and then to see my mother. The following day, I had arranged an appointment with the hospice staff, nurse, and social workers to meet at my mother's apartment in the late morning so we could go over everything. In the meantime, today was to see Mom and how her setup was in her new apartment and to start making a list of what was needed. In my purse, I had a small spiral notebook for the list-making and a couple of working pens.

As I pulled into the parking lot of her apartment complex, I found her gold sedan parked in the covered spot assigned to her apartment and I pulled in beside its assigned guest spot. I got out of the car and noticed the front end was damaged and had obviously been involved in a recent accident. She had mentioned a fender bender a couple of months earlier, but this was a bit more than a fender bender. I knocked on the first-floor apartment, which was average in every way.

I was pleased to see the new place; she had only lived in it for not even three months, and it was not completely filthy. Although it needed a good cleaning, which I already had on my list to-do. I knew my mother would have issues with me coming in and assessing what needed to be done and doing it, but we were at a point where there was no one else to do it.

I asked my mother what she wanted to do, if anything, while I was there, and we made a list of places to go. I gave her five hundred dollars in cash so that she would have enough money on hand for things she needed to buy in the next month or two. She wanted to go back to see the Casa Grande ruins that I had taken my daughters to in January. She also needed to go to Walmart to buy some things.

Once we were in the store, she quickly and adeptly obtained a motorized cart at the front. I retrieved her quad cane from the basket. She had tossed it there as if it were her purse and carried it so that she could place her items in it. She complained about how Walmart was an abusive employer and how she had been very vocal against Walmart on Facebook. She said she needed to get in and out quickly so as to not be recognized, given her Facebook feed. She continued about how she hated shopping there, but it was the cheapest place to buy everything. I heard this rhetoric of guilt every time we went to Walmart, yet we were always going to Walmart.

Back at her apartment, it was time for her to make her Essiac tea. She had wanted to get the shopping done and out of the way so she could focus on making the tea the remainder of the day. I helped her put away her purchases as she pulled out her large steel stockpot. She took an empty milk jug and filled it up with water, repeatedly dumping it into the pot until she had the amount she wanted. She was quite precise and rattled off the process from memory.

I started to notice my mother never washed her hands. She went straight from shopping, using the cart at Walmart, to touching everything, including her nose, quite frequently, and she didn't wash her hands before making the tea or her sandwich. Nor did she before she sat down to eat. She had gone to the bathroom too, and I hadn't heard any running water from the sink after the toilet flushed. She came out immediately. Afterward, she made a sandwich for herself and we watched *Little House on the Prairie* on the Hallmark Channel.

After she watched her show, she spent some time showing me her artwork. She had returned to doing some photography and was using photoshop-like software to create surrealism photography. She had several pictures framed and attempted to sell them at a market. She said she had offers, but she never sold any work because they would offer her less than the cost of materials to print. She wanted to at least break even. She seemed intent on trying to sell her artwork and was using some art platforms, and while she had views or hits, she had no sales. "I want to sell my art before I die," she said repeatedly.

It was Friday and time to meet with the staff from hospice. I had lots of questions for them, and I knew my mother didn't like me taking control of things related to her. It would be a tricky visit, but I needed to get answers and have a better understanding of where things stood and what services were provided and when. These services don't fall into place when they're needed but have to be arranged, and my mother was not in any position to have any delay in services provided.

The nurse arrived first. She already met with my mother the week prior after getting the referral from the doctor to reopen services, and the nurse was in the process of getting medications and assessing what my mother's needs would be in the near future. Surprisingly, the nurse already obtained several medications and brought them that day. They were mostly for pain, including morphine, Vicodin, naproxen, prescription dose Tylenol, and others. Basically, the strong stuff you get when you're in the hospital. A nebulizer was on order, and the nurse said when needed, they would order an oxygen tank for her to help with breathing.

I tried to speak to the nurse about the long-term care application and the medical assessment, but the nurse directed me to speak with the social workers regarding this. She was friendly enough, and my mother seemed to appreciate the attention she got from the nurse.

Shortly after her arrival, the two social workers arrived. I'm not sure why two were sent; I believe one was perhaps newer and still being trained. Now was the moment I needed to discuss future care for my mother. Hospice had an inpatient unit that she could go to, if necessary, but it was only for those last hours of life, maybe even a day or two stay, not a residential placement. The staff told me there might be some ability to send nursing staff to the apartment to provide additional, though limited, care in the home. The services that needed to be arranged were the long-term care services to provide her with placement or in-home health services prior to her qualifying for them with hospice.

As the discussion continued, my mother was becoming increasingly upset, most likely with me. She interrupted. "Excuse me. But do I not have a say in this? This is my life we're talking about."

I stopped and put on my social work/counselor hat instead of the abandoned daughter hat. "Mom," I paused and said slowly, "This is all about you. We're not trying to make decisions for you, but only trying to ensure all the things that you may need soon are being taken care of now, so they are there for you when needed."

She seemed receptive to my words, and the conversation continued. It was agreed the long-term care services would be needed. I let them know that I had planned to come back out and take a short leave to help her when she needed more assistance. Essentially referring to the end without using those words. Once it was agreed she needed the long-term care services, I told them I would contact the staff to continue the current application. One of the social workers interjected and said, "Oh, we can do that. It's our job."

My mother, being paranoid about my involvement, seemed to prefer they handle it. I hesitantly provided them with the name and number for the admission coordinator I had been dealing with and said, "If you don't continue the application and instead start a new application, it will restart the entire application process and it won't be approved in time for her needs."

They both said, "We got it," as they finished writing down the contact information I provided them. I took their names and numbers, so I now had a way to follow up. Perhaps I was at a point where I could turn over these responsibilities to someone else and simply follow up to ensure it was being taken care of.

That evening, Mom was proud to show me her favorite restaurant and what she liked about it. As we settled into the booths and waited for the food to be served, she talked about how she didn't want to be in pain. She continued with how she had heard that they can give you more morphine until you slip away and not wake up and that she wanted that when the time came. She didn't want to be in pain, and she didn't want to be alone. This was not the first occasion she mentioned both for what she hoped from her death.

The next few days passed by with a regular routine of me cleaning up a room in her house, going to a restaurant for something to eat, and going to the mall to walk. On Sunday, we went to Casa Grande, one of the things my mother wanted to do while I was there. She instantly took to the Native American flutes they sold in the gift store and decided she wanted one. It was a few hundred dollars, so I bought it for her. My mom was able to play it right away and it sounded quite nice. I'm not surprised. She always had a natural talent.

We walked throughout the museum and around the ruins that I had allowed my daughters to run around and explore. The big house was roped off, so you couldn't get inside of it, but it was interesting to see the large adobe-like building ancient Native Americans had built so many years ago. I suppose it's like the American version of the pyramids in a way.

My mother started to feel sick, and she went into the bathroom near the entrance to the museum. She handed me her cell while she was in the restroom. It rang the jungle-themed music, and the number of a bill collector appeared. She was still in the bathroom, and I could still hear her retching, most likely from all the beer she drank the day before. Her phone rang again. It was the jungle-themed music, and I didn't bother to glance at the number this time.

When my mother finally shuffled out of the bathroom, I noticed her gait was changing and she was having problems lifting her legs and instead shuffled a lot. I asked her if she wanted to leave, and she said she wasn't quite ready. She wanted to take some pictures before we left. I stood back a bit watching and snapped off a picture from behind her of her snapping a picture of the Casa Grande. She was done after that, and so was I, so we headed back to her apartment, stopping to pick up some food from the Mexican drive-through.

It was nearing the end of the visit, and today we needed to finalize the apartment. I pulled out my list and went through it to see what else, in the next couple of months, she could need. Tupperware, new dish towels, laundry detergent, cleaning supplies, soap, although she never used it. We drove to Walmart and had the same routine as last time, where she grabbed the motorized cart and went around getting supplies. She looked at little knickknacks and picked something she thought was cute for her apartment, and we picked up some fresh-cut flowers as well. We then stopped at a grocery store so she could get enough food to last her for the upcoming week. Her fridge was jam-packed again the way she liked it.

The next day was my last day there, so we decided we would see the movie at the mall. I was done attempting to finalize things for my mother. It wasn't complete, but the aggravation it caused wasn't worth the continued efforts. I drove and picked her up, and we went to lunch at the Mexican restaurant again before going to the mall.

I purchased two tickets to see the matinee of *Kung Fu Panda 2*. It was not my first choice, well, not my choice at all, but out of all the movies in the height of the summer season, this was the one she wanted to see. It's one I would have taken my kids to see, but I guess I would see it twice and enjoy a quiet couple of hours in air conditioning while slurping on a cherry Coke, my favorite. She chose seats somewhat close to the front, a little bit closer than what I was used to, but it was no matter; this was for her, and I would enjoy the peace for a bit. The movie started, and a little bit into it, I could not believe this. *What the . . . ? Are you kidding me?* I screamed in my head.

Spoiler alert if you haven't seen this movie yet, but the subplot was revealed that Po, Kung Fu Panda extraordinaire, had been abandoned by his mother, and as the story developed, it was all about him trying to find his mother and figure out why she abandoned him as a young panda. As this plot unfolded, I couldn't believe that I was watching an animated movie about a mother abandoning her child. My mother had done the same to me.

I didn't once glance over at my mother as we watched the movie. I froze in my chair. *What kind of a twisted mind did God have? What sadistic and cruel joke was this?* I pondered throughout the movie. Did I really have to go see a movie about an adult exploring why his mother abandoned him as a young child with my dying mother who abandoned me as a young child? *What the . . . ? I can't believe this* played over in my head for about two hours.

After the agonizing two hours ended, I went to the restroom, courtesy of the cherry Coke I had sucked on, trying to cope with my anxiety from the movie and to give myself a breather from my mother. We walked the mall to get her exercise in, saying not a word to each other or discussing the movie at all. We came upon a little emporium store that she wanted to look in to see some of the knickknacks, and I found myself wandering around on the opposite side of the store for about twenty minutes. I believe we both welcomed the distraction from the movie and the shift away from it. She found some frogs she liked to add to her frog knickknack collection, so I bought them for her. We resumed the walk and proceeded to discuss the items in the store that we both liked. It was a great reset, and neither of us mentioned the movie again for the rest of her short-lived days.

The next morning, I only had a few hours to spend with my mom. I had booked an early afternoon flight that would have me back home around five. I checked out of the hotel, put my luggage in the car, and headed over to Mom's for a final visit. We went to breakfast at the local diner before I headed out.

As we were heading back to her place, out of the blue, she said, "When you were around three years old, I left to go get some donuts and when I came back you were gone. When you came back, I beat the hell out of you."

I replied, "I remember."

To her amazement, I remembered the beating, but that was a beating one doesn't forget, even at such a young age. She looked at me with surprise and continued. "Why did you leave?"

I turned to her and responded, "I went to find you."

"But I woke you up and told you I was going to the store and would be right back."

I told her, "I did not know. I must have not heard you. I woke up and you were gone. I went out to find you." She forgot to mention that she also told me she ate all the donuts and had I not left I would have had one. That was the end of that discussion, once in thirty-seven years.

I made some final calls on my mother's behalf before I left. One was to the long-term care admission nurse I had been speaking to periodically for the past six months. Her voicemail clicked on, and I left a message letting her know the hospice staff would be contacting her to continue the application. The second call I placed was to Mom's social workers at hospice to do a last follow-up with them and remind them to call long-term care about continuing the current application. I also got their voicemail and left a message with the contact information for long-term care in case they misplaced it from the prior week.

A few hours later, I was home with my beautiful children in my arms. I missed them dearly.

15

I called my mother almost every day at lunchtime to see how she was doing. She was continuing with her routine of watching Hallmark, going to the mall to walk, and making her Essiac tea. The hospice nurse was coming two to three times a week to check on her, and on occasion, she was there when I called. She seemed to enjoy the visits with her. To my relief, she announced that she had quit drinking and had no intentions of drinking again. Perhaps the nurse had picked up on it and said something to her about the interaction of the medication, her illness, and the alcohol. Whatever led to the decision, I was happy to hear it. She sounded and seemed better without it.

It was now the end of July, and I had only played phone tag with the social service agencies but had not connected with anyone. Nothing really seemed to change as far as I could tell. It was hard to get a sense of what was going on when you were relying on ten-minute phone calls a few times a week.

I called the long-term care admission nurse again and got her on the phone. I told her essentially the same message a couple weeks earlier about how hospice was going to finish up the application and that I had told them to contact her and not start a new application.

She cut me off before I could finish and told me someone had submitted a new application for my mother instead of continuing with the original application we had started so many months before, and unfortunately, they would have to start the entire process over again.

My heart sank. *Why would they do that?* This desperately needed service that I worked so hard to put in place was gone. I thanked her for all her help, as she truly had gone out of her way to assist me and had stayed with me on her end for six months.

I hung up the phone, placed my face in my hands, and sobbed as I sat on the picnic bench looking over the dog park. What was I going to do now? I didn't bother calling her hospice staff to ask why they did it. There was no point. They messed it up. And I didn't call my mother and tell her either. She didn't want me involved anyways, so I left it alone. I would cross that bridge when I had to.

After I regained my composure, I called my mom to do my daily check-in with her. She proceeded to tell me she fell again. She had now a handful of falls that I had known about and probably a handful more that I did not. She was walking outside the apartment and fell, but this time she couldn't get back up. She tried calling out for help, and even some of the residents walked by and she asked them to help her up, but they wouldn't. They walked right past, ignoring her. She was on the ground in the height of the heat of the summer day for about fifteen minutes. After a few people ignored her request for help, some guys came by and helped her up and to her apartment. I suggested she call her nurse to let them know, but she said she didn't want to. I would have called, but her paranoia had returned with a vengeance, so I receded and left it alone. I didn't know what to do at this point.

16

August 2011

That bridge came to be crossed sooner than I expected that next week. I received a call from my mother telling me she was in hospice's care at their inpatient facility. She went to her appointment with her oncologist that morning and was sent to hospice's in-patient facility and was subsequently admitted. I tried to understand what happened, but it didn't make sense to me. She was scared. I asked to let me call her oncologist again to speak with them and her hospice social worker and she said, "Yeah. Okay."

I called the doctor's office and was able to get a nurse on the line. She told me my mother had come to see the doctor and appeared very confused and disoriented, so he sent her to the hospice unit. There was not much else for them to tell me nor for them to do for her. She had lung cancer, but it was also in her brain, and this was not an unusual turn for her to take.

I called her social worker but only received their voicemail. I left a message. I then called the hospice unit she was admitted to and spoke with the staff assigned. They told me she would stay a day or two at most, but then would be discharged back home.

I dialed Mom's cell number again and asked her again what they told her. She couldn't tell me why she was sent there and didn't understand beyond her oncologist sent her and they admitted her. She knew she would be there for a couple of days.

"Mom, I think it's time you come here and stay with me."

She paused for a moment. Earlier in the year, the discussion to move where I was had been declined. This time she conceded and said, "Okay."

"Let me see how to arrange this and I'll call you back tomorrow. It'll be okay, Mom." I didn't believe it and I doubt she did either. I had hope that it would, she had quit drinking and that was of upmost importance for her coming to stay with my children. I could and would not have her yelling and screaming at them. That was my only rule.

A few days later, I flew out to Arizona. The car was already packed with what she was bringing, and some items were boxed up and shipped to the house and were arriving about a week later. It was not but a few hours after I landed at the airport that we were on the road heading back to Florida. Mom watched the speedometer religiously to ensure we weren't going too fast. When she drove, it was always at least ten under the speed limit at her fastest. I wondered why she drove so slowly. Was it a habit and she that cautious of a driver? I found that hard to fathom. Perhaps it was the major car accident she was involved in when I was a child. She was in a full leg cast, from what I remember.

When I arrived at my mother's, a reality check set in. She was highly agitated, having a lot of difficulty walking, and her balance was shot. In the past, I had worked with elderly patients and had learned over the years many techniques to "walk with assistance," meaning you guide them to walk where you want them to go. I modified these techniques and came up with a way to take her arm in mine, but such that I provided her support and direction when she started to fall or lose her balance. This was how we walked everywhere together for the entire drive home across seven states.

17

We drove, stopping every few hours, making our way out of Arizona through New Mexico and into Texas. It was an easy enough drive to take, as I-10 stretched all the way from Arizona into Florida. Once in Florida, it was a straight shot home on familiar roads through cities and towns after we got through the panhandle. At least I would be able to add all the states I had visited to my travel list.

We stopped somewhere in Texas around San Antonio that first night after having put in a good twelve-hour drive on top of me flying from Ft. Lauderdale to Phoenix. Mom had a sandwich in the room, but I was exhausted and had no appetite, so I ate nothing. She showered and so did I, and we went to bed. The parking lot light filtered into the room enough to where I could see Mom in her bed, the one closest to the bathroom in case she had to get up. Despite the light making its way past the blackout curtains, I fell right to sleep.

It must have been a couple of hours, but it felt like minutes when I heard my mother moving in her bed. I forced open my eyes to see she was getting up, and I turned to see if she needed help. Her gait was so unsteady, I worried she would fall and hit her head. I got up and walked her to the bathroom until she grabbed ahold of the wall and then worked her way toward the toilet, steadying herself on the vanity next to it. I closed the door to give her privacy and waited near the door. I heard the flush of the toilet and then a moment later the door pushed open. She didn't bother to wash or even rinse her hands. I helped her back to bed and then I fell right back to sleep but was conscious to listen for my mother.

What seemed like a few minutes later, I heard my mother rustling around in the bed and forced myself once again to open my eyes. I was so tired. *Okay, here we go again to the bathroom.* I turned my head in the direction of the other bed. I blinked a couple times as I adjusted my eyes. I continued to hear the rustling of the sheets. She was not getting out of bed this time. As it became clear to me what she was doing, she looked directly at me, her eyes wide, staring directly into mine. The sheet moved repeatedly around the middle of the bed, rustling in unison to the movement of her hand as she continued to satisfy herself while staring directly into my eyes. She didn't stop. *Oh, God. Really?* I thought to myself as I rolled over. I quickly closed my eyes and fell back to sleep.

It was around seven when I woke up to the phone ringing. It was the wake-up call. I got up, and my mother began to speak about the night before. I looked away, headed to the bathroom and, placed my hand in her direction, waving off the discussion about why she was satisfying herself with me in the room and why she didn't stop when she knew I was awake and aware of what she was doing. I was not going to have this conversation with her . . . ever. The look in her eyes will haunt me forever. It was bad enough she did this, but the fact that she didn't stop when she knew I was awake and aware was what bothered me most. I was becoming extremely anxious about how she would behave when we were home with my children. She had calmed down some since they gave her Depakote and she wasn't drinking, but her behavior was still erratic and concerning. I would not have my children terrorized by her, and I was concerned this was where we were heading. On top of all this, she never washed her hands. Why wouldn't she wash her hands?

Back on the road, my mother noticed a sign for the Alamo about an hour or so away and made a comment how she had never been and it would be interesting to see. I would have liked to have stopped too, but we couldn't. We had to get back. My mother's life was at its end, but life still had to go on. I had children to tend to and work. I couldn't pick up and go on a road trip with her, although I thought that it wasn't a bad idea to drive forever with her until she passed away. Sort of a *Thelma & Louise* meets *Terms of Endearment* meets *Misery* menagerie. I think in some respects that was what she wanted. I would have liked to have given that to her, but I couldn't.

Texas was a long drive, but we made our way into Louisiana and drove through New Orleans. It was a relatively quiet drive, mostly listening to music peppered with an occasional comment or observation about the sights. An occasional interruption to stop for a bathroom break where my mother would simply place her hands under the running water of the tap for a second, if even that long, before exiting the facilities. The music she played changed from seventies rock to Native American flute music. My mom had introduced me to R. Carlos Nakai's melancholic sounds of the wood flute. It was peaceful and serene. It was what I needed and thought Mom could benefit from it too.

We drove until around eight in the evening and landed in the panhandle, stopping at a hotel off the interstate. We ate and

I showered; Mom did not, which was probably a good thing. I hadn't thought about it at the time, but she most likely couldn't get in or out of the bathtub. I'm glad she didn't try. It was early when we went to bed. She put on the TV, but I went to sleep.

The phone rang again at around seven with the wake-up call, and we packed up and hit the road. We drove through Tallahassee, an area my mother had lived in for several years after leaving me in Gainesville, and then toward Lake City, where we merged onto I-75. We stopped at an Arby's on the way. My mother saw the sign and had a hankering for a beef cheddar sandwich, so we pulled through the drive-through and headed on toward Gainesville.

Oddly enough, neither of us discussed Gainesville as we drove past it. I looked past the three major exits that I had grown to know so well, living there until I was five years old and again as a student, and saw how much the area had continued to develop. A couple hours later, we were on the turnpike for the last leg of the trip. It was all very familiar now driving past Orlando where my grandmother, her mother, lived. I hadn't hardly spoken with my grandmother since learning of my mother's illness at the beginning of the year, even though I would normally visit her at least a few times a year. My mother didn't want my grandmother to know she was ill, and she became very paranoid of my relationship with her and that I was talking to her mother about her. I wasn't, but I simply didn't speak with my grandmother anymore as my mother's illness had progressed. Things were too difficult anyways. I had nothing I wanted to share with her at this time.

18

It was around seven in the evening when we made it home. I scooped up my children in my arms as my mother took in the house she would be living in, and I showed her to her room. She took no notice of her grandchildren and showed no interest in them. Her belongings were placed in my bedroom, which was now her room and bathroom since it was the only one downstairs. I would sleep on the couch for the time being.

My mother was almost out of her Essiac tea, so the first thing she wanted to do was make a pot of it. But I needed to buy some supplies for her to make it in, so we decided to focus on that the next day. My mom made herself comfortable, pulling off her wig, a synthetic store-bought one, not the one made of her own hair, and sat in the ideal viewing spot on the couch with the remote in hand watching the Hallmark Channel while I took care of the girls' dinner and then their bath, trying to maintain their routine. Tomorrow would be a busy day.

I woke at seven in the morning to get the girls up and fed. We started a little bit later than usual since I wasn't going into work. The girls had a couple of days left and then it was their break week. We were supposed to be going to the Keys for a respite, but now we were staying home, and I would have to manage my mother being around the children for the week they were off. No matter. I had the day at hand to focus on. I got the girls out the door and left my mother at the house.

I had arranged a Life Alert for her for those times she would be left on her own. There was no way I could supervise her every minute of the day and would sometimes have to leave her on her own when tending to my children. There was a necklace part to it, like on the commercials, and another one for when you left the house that clipped on to your belt.

The school was literally a block behind the house if you walked out of the backyard and through the small preserve behind it, but we drove, so it was slightly farther, yet still only a couple minutes' drive. I dropped them off and sat in the car for a few minutes to ready myself for the day at hand with my mother.

I drove back after being gone from the house less than ten minutes, and I found my mother sprawled out on the floor in the kitchen next to the refrigerator. She no longer had the strength to get herself up. I asked her why she didn't use her Life Alert, and she said she figured I would be back at some point. She really didn't like the idea of the Life Alert, and I don't blame her for this, but I suppose if it were truly dire, she would use it. No matter, she was okay.

The local hospice nurse would be by that afternoon to assess what she needed and do the intake for their unit, so we would mention it then. She was starting to fall more, though I was usually there to catch her before she went down. I reached under her arms and pulled her up to her feet, keeping her weight in my arms until she could regain her balance. She leaned some on the counter and then I walked her to the couch. She was trying to get herself some Essiac tea. I poured her some and gave it to her on the couch in her newfound spot.

I made a list while she watched *Little House on the Prairie* and drank her tea. We needed to buy a stockpot; its sole purpose would be for her Essiac tea. We also needed a strainer and a container for her to keep it in. We also needed her basic supplies of toothpaste and shampoo, even though she only had stubble on her head.

I ran a concurrent list of what to discuss with the nurse too. She needed a chair for the shower, a walker, or a wheelchair. A four-pronged cane was not enough support for her. Medications for her mood, really for paranoia. She watched me relentlessly as if I were up to something. She wasn't wrong. I was up to something. I was trying to balance everything as best I could, and that was it. But it felt like she was suspicious of me. *Perhaps I should ask for more medication for me too for my suspiciousness of her suspiciousness of me.* I chuckled and shook my head.

I finished up the list, grabbed my stuff, and helped her to the car. We went to a nearby Walmart. I parked the car near the second entrance to avoid a lot of traffic and give her a closer spot to the door. She used her quad cane today, but I still walked on her other side to hold her up.

We were at the entrance and the greeter helped us find a motorized cart. It was a super Walmart, and it was big. She was a bit in awe, like a kid in a candy store, and she turned her head from side to side, taking in the size of it. It was probably twenty-five percent larger than the one she was used to. We got everything she needed, and a few hundred dollars later we were set.

Back at home, she showed me how to make the Essiac tea.

"Pour in the water with the tea scooped into the pot and bring it to a boil while stirring it every ten minutes and then let it simmer in the pot, stirring minimally every two hours," she instructed me.

It would have to sit there until two a.m. and then be poured into the container after being strained and then placed in the fridge. So, we set a timer to stir it in a couple of hours.

The nurse would be there shortly, so Mom sat on the couch while I went upstairs to the computer to tend to my work. Today I would check my emails and try to catch up on some things before they got too far behind. My mother shuffled periodically, going back and forth from the couch in the family room to the front door looking out the peephole. As I heard her moving around, I called down to her, "Mom, is everything alright?"

She replied, "Yeah. It's fine. I'm looking out the door. Your dog won't move, though. I'm afraid she's going to trip me." She was referring to my then fifteen-year-old dog that I had had since college who had become more and more of a rug lying on the rug at the front door. She had a dog bed that she used at night, but she spent her day in front of the door asleep on the rug.

"She's old, Mom. That's her spot." I yelled back down to her.

The nurse arrived shortly after, and she introduced herself and started asking for my mother's medical history. My mother lied to her and told her she had never used illicit drugs. She said the same about alcohol consumption. I turned and moved around in the kitchen, cleaning up the Essiac tea mess. The nurse began with her intake as I left them to be alone in the living room. My mother really didn't want me to be a part of this, and I wasn't going to push the issue.

When the nurse came to find me to ask me some questions, my mother followed her. I directed her to my mother because I could tell my mother did not like her talking with me. I gave occasional input about her needs when the nurse said they would order supplies like she had in Phoenix. A nebulizer for breathing treatments and an oxygen tank. I really didn't like the idea of an oxygen tank in the house, but she felt it would be needed. She would order more pain medication and increase the dosage of morphine. My mom really didn't take the pain medications, but she was ordering what the usual list would include.

I asked her for the shower chair, walker, and wheelchair and discussed my mother's falls. The nurse said we should call her each time she falls to have her evaluated. She had fallen every day, and my mother and I agreed on one thing—that we were not going to call each time she fell to have someone come to the house to assess her. The nurse then suggested she come with her to stay a night or two at the inpatient hospital unit for an evaluation. My mother looked at me for input, and I wasn't going to push her to go.

My mother went into her room to retrieve some things and while she did, I asked the nurse if the doctor could assess my mother to increase her dosage of Depakote. It was not as effective for her mood as it had been, and I thought she could benefit from an increase in the medication or some other medication.

The nurse stopped writing and looked at me with pause stating, "The Depakote is prescribed as preventive for seizures, not mood."

I said I understood and that it was helping her mood, but it wasn't working as well to stabilize it as it had been and if the doctor could assess this. The nurse looked at me and said nothing further.

I thought to myself, *Seriously? Has this nurse never dealt with someone who is psychiatrically compromised?*

My mother came out of the bedroom with a small rolling suitcase behind her. She sat on the couch and the nurse continued to explain what they would do with her in the facility to assess her. My mom was hesitant to go, and I wasn't going to force the issue. I simply reiterated that it was a temporary stay so they could monitor her and see what her needs were. I added, "But this is your decision; if you don't want to go, you don't have to, and if you want to and don't like it, you can call me, and I will come pick you up."

She said, "Yes," and a sense of relief washed over me. Perhaps they would see her mood and give her something to help her depression, anxiety, mania, and psychotic thinking. Any one of them would do.

The nurse took Mom to the nearby hospice unit. I could only hope that the staff and doctor would see what I told the nurse and give her medication to help her relax.

For the first time in a while, I had time to sit by myself. I had to pick up the girls from school in a half hour, but it was a half hour to myself, alone. I sat on the couch as I began to process the enormity of what had happened in the past several months and how it continued to escalate washed over me in waves, each wave bigger than the one before. My eyes welled up with tears as I sobbed uncontrollably. *Why won't it stop? Why can't these people work with me?* I clamped my eyes shut and stopped the emotions from cascading further into an avalanche. I didn't have time to deal with them. I stuffed them back inside, wiped my eyes, sucked in a huge breath of air, and released it. I rose from the couch, grabbed my purse and keys, and went to pick up my children.

I was giving the girls a snack when my mother called. She had forgotten her toothbrush and a few other things. She told me she really didn't like it there and asked if she should stay. I said the same thing I had said to her before, trying to be as neutral as possible. I reminded her again if she decided she didn't want to stay, I could come pick her up. I told her I could either come now with the girls or later in the evening after they were in bed. She chose to wait until I could come alone. It saddened me that she could find no joy in having grandchildren.

I was getting ready to leave and called my mom to let her know I was on my way and if there was anything else she wanted me to bring. She asked for a chocolate shake, so I stopped at the ice-cream shop around the corner from the house to have an authentic one made for her. About twenty minutes later, I was at the facility.

It looked like a typical small hospital or nursing home on the outside, and it was nestled in a nook of Florida vegetation. Inside was a long hallway of offices that were now empty and dark. I went to the nurse's station and asked the nurse what room my mom was in. The nurse looked it up in the computer and pointed me around the corner and down the hall on the left. She directed me to sign in on the opened spiral book on the desk.

I headed down the hall and heard some voices in some of the other rooms. I knocked on the door as I pushed it open to reveal my mother in bed with the TV on. She looked up at me and said, "Hi." I continued into the room and held up my hands, revealing the bag of items she requested.

"I have your stuff," I said.

She replied, "Oh, great." I handed her the shake and placed the bag on top of the small dresser across from the bed. She sucked immediately on the straw, inhaling the shake. She talked about the shake, how good it was, in between taking large sips and swallowing. "You can tell the difference between a malt and a regular shake," she said. "It's so much better. Richer." She continued to suck on the straw.

I sat in the chair next to the bed looking around the room, taking it all in as I simply replied, "Hmm-mm," as I nodded. The room she was in was sort of depressing. It was a cream-colored shade, not quite tan, but not quite yellow either and seemed rather dated. The furniture was sparse and typical for a hospital. A small TV was mounted in the corner closer to the ceiling, which I suppose made it easier to watch reclined in bed.

I stayed for a bit until about eleven. I placed the gallon of Essiac tea in the fridge and left the facility. It was quiet with not much activity both inside and out.

A couple of hours later, my phone rang, waking me from a deep sleep. I could barely open my eyes I was so tired and so soundly asleep. I opened the phone and answered it before it went to voicemail.

It was my mom. "I want to come home," she said. "I don't want to be here."

I heard the fear in her voice and replied, "Okay. I'm on my way and will be there in a little bit."

When I got to the hospital, I told the nurse at the front desk I was there to pick up my mother and that she had called me to get her. She told me in order for my mother to be discharged, we had to wait for the doctor on call. I went to my mother's room and explained they needed to call the doctor to get permission to discharge.

My mother became a little irritated at this and said, "Let's go." She already had everything packed up, and she was dressed in her clothes.

I knew facilities had discharge policies and, in my disorientation, while I was trying to awaken from the much-needed sleep, I hadn't thought about the facility's discharge policy. I told her, "Let's give them a few minutes. It's their policy."

The nurse came in to speak with my mother, who was becoming more agitated. The nurse quickly retreated, trying to calm my mother by stating, "Okay. I understand, but we need to do a discharge. Let me call my supervisor back. Give me a few minutes." My mother settled on the bed, still with her purse in her hand, waiting to leave. I sat waiting for the nurse to return to see what the response would be and wondered if they would try to further dissuade her or if they would let her go without any further issues.

Luckily, the nurse returned and asked my mother to sign a discharge paper, which she did, and we left without further issue. My mother never saw the doctor, never got additional medication for anything, much less her mood, and she was now more agitated and anxious.

About three hours after we arrived home, my alarm went off, and I had to get up to tend to the girls. I tried to keep them quiet so they wouldn't wake my mother. But the kitchen and eating area were right next to the bedroom, and they were three years old. She woke up and came out and sat on the couch, wanting to turn the channel on the TV from the Mickey Mouse Clubhouse to I don't know what. I asked her to wait so the girls could watch their show while we finished getting ready. She sat on the couch not saying anything, looking impatient at having to wait to watch her shows. I tried to hurry up and even left a few minutes early with the girls to remove them from being around my mother. Before I left, I handed my mother the Life Alert button with the lanyard to put around her neck. She placed it on the coffee table in front of her and changed the channel to the Hallmark Channel.

I drove the girls to school and made sure I had my cell phone nearby and that the ringer was turned on. We sat in the car in the parking lot for a few minutes before we went inside because we were a little too early.

My anxiety was heightening with how things were going. I worried mostly for the upcoming week with the girls being at home every day since their preschool would be closed for the summer vacation week. My intention was to take my mother out of the house or have the girls out of the house the majority of the time to limit her exposure to them, so they didn't annoy her and she didn't lash out at them. However, we were going to have a few days where the four of us were together. There wasn't any way around it, and I worried about this.

I was gone about fifteen minutes, returned and opened the door. I heard my name being called from the other room and found my mother on the floor in the kitchen yet again. The Life Alert was still on the coffee table. I put my purse down on the counter and bent to her on the floor, placing both my arms under hers, gently lifting her to her feet.

All the while she was explaining in an irritated voice, "You left my Essiac tea at that place and so I needed to make some more."

"Yes, Mom. I didn't even think of the tea last night."

She continued, "That was the only tea I had so I need to make some more. When I bent down to get the pot out of the cabinet, I fell forward and hit my head."

"I'm sorry, Mom, about the tea. I wish I had remembered to get it." I meant it. I really wished I had remembered, but I didn't. I helped her to the couch and asked, "Do you want me to call the nurse to tell her about the fall?"

"No," she snapped. "I don't want you to call the nurse about the fall."

I didn't argue with her. I didn't want to call the nurse either. *Bonanza* was on now, and she started to watch it as I said, "Mom, why don't you let me make the tea for you?"

She responded without taking her gaze from the TV screen. "You don't know how."

"Well, Mom, why don't you walk me through it so I learn how. You might need me to make it for you at some point, so why don't you show me how now?"

She mumbled in acknowledgment, "Yeah. I suppose I will need you to make it at some point."

She walked me through the steps, and I boiled the exact amount of water and then added the exact amount of the herbal tea blend in loose leaf form to the boiling water. I stirred it as I watched it float around at the top of the water, turning a dark color as the water permeated the herbs. I placed the lid on the stockpot and pushed it to the back of the stove to simmer for an hour or so, stirring it every fifteen minutes.

My mother's phone rang, and it was hospice staff, another nurse than the one who had come out the previous day. I could hear my mother on the phone with them, and then she yelled out to me, "Hospice wants to come out again today."

To which I responded, "Okay."

She held the phone out in my direction and said, "Here. They want to speak to you." I wiped my hands off with the dishtowel, walked over, and took the phone from her. The nurse said she would come out later today to further assess Mom and that social workers would also call to arrange an intake for their part. I wouldn't be able to take Mom out of the house until the new hospice nurse came. I could hear Mom pacing downstairs like a caged animal. She shuffled back and forth from the couch to the front window and now and then to the kitchen to stir the pot of Essiac tea while she waited for the nurse to show. I went downstairs, and shortly thereafter, the nurse arrived.

They sat in the family room off of the kitchen, and I let them speak alone while I sat in the front living room. I went into the kitchen when the Essiac tea needed to be stirred, and the nurse spoke to both of us about what she was going to order for my mother. She was ordering more pain pills, including morphine, to supplement what my mother already had in addition to the other medications. She was ordering her an oxygen tank in addition to a nebulizer. My mother never used the nebulizer when she had it in Arizona, but the nurse was insistent and told me I was to make her use it.

There was no chance I would be insisting my mother use or take anything. I would ensure she took her Depakote on schedule, though, to try to keep her mood stable in addition to the seizures and remind her about all her medication times, but the rest I would not be ensuring she took if she refused them and didn't want to. She had so many pills to take and so many times a day.

We again discussed the falling, and the nurse said she would order her a walker and a wheelchair. I was very thankful for that, as my mother really needed them. The medications and equipment would arrive later that afternoon.

The nurse continued that the doctor and a social worker would come out to see her the next week to further evaluate her needs. I listened but didn't ask questions or say much unless a question was directed to me, and even then, I would direct the question back to my mother. No one seemed to pick up on that my mother didn't want me involved and it irritated her each time staff spoke to me about her.

The next day was Saturday, and the girls were up early, around seven, as always. I knew my mother would be out soon, as the girls tried to be as quiet as three-year-olds can be. The girls had their breakfast, and I got them dressed. They watched

Mickey Mouse, and shortly thereafter, my mother came out of her room. I made her some breakfast and sat with her in the dining room while the girls stayed in the family room watching TV. I told my mother we could go out of the house shortly and discussed what she wanted to do for the day. My ex would stay with the girls while I spent the day with my mother. I was exhausted and wanted to stay in bed, but the sooner I got her out of the house, the better it was for me, my kids, and her. If I could keep her entertained and away from the girls while she still had energy, it might work out.

She said she wanted to go down to Hollywood Beach. She used to go there as a teenager all the time and she wanted to see it again. Hollywood beach was literally at the opposite end of the county we lived in, but we had plenty of time. It took about an hour to make it to the boardwalk area and then I had to find a place to park where I could pull out her wheelchair. Unfortunately, we didn't have a handicap decal to park in the designated spots. Fortunately, I had the minivan, which provided plenty of room for her wheelchair. I pulled the van into a spot, giving my mother some extra room to get out of the car, and I helped her to her wheelchair in the back of the car.

We walked a few blocks south and came to the Arts Park Amphitheater, which was empty beyond a few people sitting in some of the rows resting or taking a break from their beach excursion. I pushed her chair down the walk, navigating around others who were not paying attention. My mom didn't seem to really notice the challenge either. She stared out toward the sand and the ocean and turned her head back to the stores and the people we passed. Some walked past us, and others rolled by on bikes and Rollerblades. It was a bit of a workout pushing her down the boardwalk in the heat of the day in the middle of

August, which was the beginning of the most horrendous time of year weather-wise in South Florida. The humidity was at its maximum now, and sweat poured off of me. The last chance before school resumed people flocked to the beach.

We walked for over an hour, and my mom spotted a Häagen Dazs ice-cream store on the boardwalk and wanted a chocolate shake—a malted one if they had it. They had a couple of small metal tables outside that were shaded by the canopy in front of the store. Fortunately, one off to the side was empty, so I pulled her chair next to the table and faced her looking out toward the walk and the beach beyond it so she could enjoy the view while I went in. I bought two bottles of water and a chocolate malted shake for her. She slurped on her shake while I rested and drank the entire water bottle.

We continued the walk for about a half hour longer and reached another area that had an outdoor patio area with seating. I was getting quite tired from pushing her down the boardwalk and needed to rest again. We sat for a while, in no hurry to rush back. I had to push her all the way back to the car, and I would take my time doing it to allow more time to pass before we returned to the house where my mom would be around the girls.

We were about halfway back to the car when my mom finally spoke and said, "I bet I could walk to the water."

I was horrified at the prospect of her trying to walk in the sand. It was hard enough to walk in the sand without balance issues, but she was in a wheelchair now; there was no way she could walk on the beach, much less all the way down to the water. "Mom, there's no way you're getting down to the water. You'll fall."

She started to argue with me and replied, "I bet I could."

I responded, "Mom, there's no way, and I can't carry you."

She nodded her head in agreement and then said, "We can use the chair."

I retorted, "Mom. I know you want to go to the water, but I can't push you in the chair, and I can't carry you either. I wish that I could get you to the water, but I can't, and you'll end up stuck in the sand and unable to get up, and I don't know that I can manage getting you back out of the sand. It's too much."

She began to open her mouth as the word "but" started to come out and then she conceded. There was no way she was going to make it to the water, and she knew that. I took one more much-needed break on the way back to the car, then I loaded my mom up, and off we went. On the way out, I took a longer way home so we could drive near the ocean along the strip. That was the last time my mother would ever see the ocean.

Now it was Sunday, and it was raining. This would make it quite difficult to do anything that day, and tomorrow it was her and I with the girls all day. My ex had a few days off at the end of the week, but the first half would be us. I spent most of the day entertaining the girls upstairs in the loft or in their room to keep some distance from my mother as she watched TV. She commented on the rain and how it had been such a long time since she had seen rain like this. South Florida was nearing the height of the hurricane season. Most rainy days in Florida are afternoon showers that roll off the Everglades and last for an hour or two and then by evening it's sunny out again.

I was exhausted both mentally and physically, and the upcoming week was going to be particularly challenging for me with the girls being home with Mom for the entire day. My mother would have to spend time with them. She had wanted to get a small desk to put in the room so she could sit with her computer when it arrived later in the week. I think she missed it, and I was looking forward to it coming as well so that she might have something to occupy her time with other than watching TV when we were in the house. It would be good for her and good for me because she would be off to herself away from the kids some, which would eliminate some of her agitation.

"I thought tomorrow we could go with the girls to the office supply store and buy you a desk," I said.

"Okay. I'd like to do that."

I continued, "There's a store near the house, then I can put it together for you when we get home."

Since we would have the girls today, I opted to bring the walker for her to use in the store in addition to the wheelchair in the minivan.

The girls climbed into the minivan and jumped into their seats as I helped my mother down the step outside of the house and then into the front seat. I helped her buckle in and then finished buckling in each of my daughters into their car seats.

My daughters were still at the end of a cold, and each of them sneezed a couple of times. My mother had a look of horror on her face. Not an unusual reaction, I supposed, when confronted with one's own mortality. I had told her before I brought her here that the girls and I had been fighting either a cold or a virus of some sort and that we were all on medications. I reminded her of this.

"You know," she commented, "I could catch what they have, and it could kill me."

"I know, Mother. I've been trying to keep them away from you as much as possible so you won't catch it. I took them to the doctor for you, and they have been on medication for over a week now and are almost finished with it. I don't think they or I are contagious at this point, but there's nothing I can do about it. If you aren't comfortable, then I can take us back to the house instead of us going out to get your desk."

She quickly responded, "No. Let's go to the store. I want to get the desk."

We spent about an hour at the store, which was perfect for the girls to run out some energy. Mom did really well with her walker, so I was able to keep the girls a good distance away from her most of the time. She picked out a small computer desk, and we paid for it and headed home.

The girls no longer took naps, which was rather unfortunate. This would have been nap time and provided Mom with a break from the girls. Instead, I decided to enlist the girls' help in assembling the desk. I pulled the box into the bedroom, and the girls came in with me while Mom stayed out in the family room watching her shows. We pulled all the pieces out of the box and the girls helped me screw in the components.

Mom's computer was supposed to come today, and I could hear her getting up from the couch and shuffling to the window to look out and then returning to the couch at each commercial break. Occasionally, she would come to the bedroom door and look in at us working on her desk.

"They aren't going to get into my stuff, are they?" she asked.

"No, Mom. They're not going into your closet or near your stuff. They're helping me put together your desk." She went back to the couch and came back periodically to look at the progress on the desk.

You could see she was upset that I was taking so long to put the desk together because of the girls' involvement. We continued, and eventually the girls and I completed. About an hour later, Mom's computer was delivered in the mail. Mom wanted to be part of this install, so we reversed roles, and the girls watched

TV out in the living room while I hooked my mother's computer up so that she could use it.

Mom was now on the internet, which was great. It would provide another activity for her inside the house to occupy her time when I was unable to tend to her. I was off from work this week, but I would have to spend time working from the house starting next week. My mother was going to have to understand I would not be at her beck and call to entertain her. I know she wanted to fill her last days with adventures and activities, and if I could have, I would have done that with her, but my life had to continue, and that included taking care of my children and my job.

Thankfully, the next few days passed rather uneventfully. My mother had another meeting with her social workers, during which she asked to resume cancer treatment. I reminded her that being treated again would require her to be discharged from hospice, which meant that she would no longer qualify for their services. Fortunately, she didn't argue and responded half-heartedly, "Yes, I understand."

19

It was Friday, August 19, 2011, and we were in the homestretch of the girls' school break. It was drizzling outside, so I couldn't take the girls or Mom for a walk to the lake as we had been doing. I was going to take my mom out to get her away from the girls, but for some reason, she was extra agitated today. She said she couldn't find her Waterpik toothbrush nor her electric razor and proceeded to blame the girls. I told her the girls hadn't been in the room and there was no way they could've taken them, but she was insistent they took them from her room.

She yelled and screamed, and I told her, "Mom, I told you, you can't yell and scream at the girls." She kept going, escalating louder, and I told her, "Mom, stay in the room until you can calm down." I closed the door, and the girls were in the family room watching TV. My mother came railing out of the room yelling and cursing in front of the girls before I had a chance to move them to another part of the house. They began to cry, sobbing as their grandmother called them "little brats." I turned her around, walked her into the bedroom again, and closed the door. "Don't come out until you're calm, Mother. You can't yell at my kids like that. I told you that. The one thing I said was, 'you cannot yell at my kids;' they're only three years old."

I walked out, not waiting for a response, and went to my girls and held them, giving them kisses and telling them, "It's okay. Grandma is sick and doesn't know what she's saying." I removed them from the area to avoid further confrontations with my mother.

The girls calmed down, and I headed to the kitchen phone to call the social worker to come and get my mother. I was able to have the staff page the social workers, and they called back. I explained what happened and said they needed to come get her. She couldn't stay with me any longer. I couldn't risk my children's welfare.

The hospice staff and the doctor arrived about an hour later to reevaluate my mother. The doctor sat in the family room with my mother, and I could hear her complaining about me and my children. I told the social worker gently and matter-of-factly, "My mother lied to you. She has an extensive drug and alcohol history. She left when I was young and wasn't around when I was growing up. I was trying to take care of her while she was in her final days, as she had no other options, but my one issue was my children. I told her she couldn't yell and scream at them, and she did. I can't keep her here. She wrongly blamed them, and I can't risk their well-being." She told me an ambulance was on the way to pick her up and take her to the hospital unit that she had been in the week before. I let the social worker know that she didn't like it there.

Every so often, my mother would raise her voice as she was insulting me to the doctor so it was loud enough for me to hear. "That's probably why she's so fat," she said to the doctor and the social worker looked at me.

I shook my head in disbelief.

The doctor left, and about an hour later, the social worker asked if it would be all right if she left too.

"It's fine," I said. My mother had been quiet in the bedroom since the doctor left, and there were no current issues.

On her way out, the social worker said, "The ambulance should be here within the hour to pick her up."

About a half hour later, the ambulance arrived, having backed the vehicle to the door so the double doors would open right to the front door. Two large men came in with a stretcher and helped her onto it. She looked at me as I watched her being wheeled out and placed into the ambulance. I simply closed the door once she was in it. I didn't say a word to her, and she said nothing to me.

20

I felt conflicted. Relief, hurt, bewilderment, disbelief at all I had been through that year, and probably a bit numb. It was just one more moment of drama that didn't need to occur and certainly not how I wanted things to go.

Over the weekend, I moved my belongings back into my bedroom. I didn't hear a word from my mother or the staff at hospice. While reorganizing the room with the assistance of someone, she looked under the bathroom sink and found another steak knife wedged into the plastic storage caddy. My mother had taken the knife blade and cut the plastic so that it stood up with the handle ready to grab. As she showed me the discovery, she said, "It looks like your mother was going to kill you in your sleep." I had the same thought as she said it. It took some effort on her part to dislodge the knife from the container. I looked at it for a moment and shook my head again and put it in the dishwasher.

After a few days of hearing nothing, my phone rang, and it was my mother. I paused for a moment and then answered it, surprised that she was calling me. "Hello," I said in a matter-of-fact tone.

She responded back, "Hi." She spoke as if nothing had taken place between us and asked if I could bring her some socks, underwear, clothes, and her Essiac tea.

I wrote down what she needed on an old list I pulled out of my purse. "I'll bring it up to you in about a couple of hours when I can leave the house."

She said, "Okay," and before we hung up, I asked her if there was anything else she wanted. She asked for a chocolate shake, preferably a malt.

"Okay," I said. "There's an ice cream shop around the corner, and I'll stop there on my way." I packed up some clothes in a plastic bag and any other items I thought she might want or need.

When I was able to leave, I drove to the ice-cream store around the corner, ordered the chocolate malt, and then drove the twenty minutes to the facility. It was off the highway and conveniently located.

I walked into the facility, which was so oddly quiet, and went to the desk. I told them who I was and signed into the visitor's log. The staff told me the room number my mother was in and pointed down the corridor perpendicular to the one she had been in the last time.

I found the room about halfway down the corridor and knocked on the door as I pushed it open. "Hello. Mom?" I said as I walked past the bathroom.

She lay in the bed, propped up and watching TV. "Hi," she replied, looking at me as I came in.

I handed her the chocolate shake and placed the bag of clothes on the chair. "I brought the stuff you asked for."

"Oh, great." She sucked on the shake. "Oh, there's nothing like a malted shake. It's so much better than a regular shake."

I nodded and grinned in acknowledgment. As I sat down, I looked around the room. She had two French doors that led out to a covered porch area with a beautiful grand three-tiered water fountain in the middle of the backyard. I thought it was quite lovely and commented. "This is a nice view you have from this room, Mom."

She concurred and said, "Yes. It's much better than the last time." She paused for a moment. "Can I come home?"

I could not take her back with my children. It wasn't safe. Maybe when she was at a place where she was more subdued, but not the way she was behaving. "I can't have you around the girls, Mom. Besides, it's not good for you, either. You shouldn't have to be around three-year-olds."

"Yeah," she replied. "I told you that."

She hadn't, but I wasn't going to argue with her. I tried my best, but if she came home now, it was going to end up with someone getting seriously injured. She was hiding knives and was going to hurt me or my children, and I couldn't risk that. Her paranoia was too much, and no one yet could see it. Had they given her some medication, it might have worked out.

"They're going to put me into a nursing home."

"I know that, Mom." I knew when she came here that would be what they did next. They will try to stick her in some terrible nursing home in the area. Her only saving grace was that it would take some time to find and make arrangements for a placement, in which case it might be too late.

"I tell you what, Mom," I said. "If you want me to help you find placement, tell the staff here to call me and I'll work with them on it." I knew she wouldn't have the staff call me. She had vilified me in all this and that would require her telling them the truth, or at least some part of it. She didn't answer, which I expected. I broke the silence. "I can visit you here and bring you what you need at lunchtime and some nights after work if you would like."

"Okay," she said. "My clothes are dirty."

"I'll do your laundry and bring back your clean clothes in a couple days so you have enough." She told me she wanted a laptop and that she would like a hamburger for lunch the next day. I replied, "Okay, Mom. I'll pick up Wendy's on the way at lunchtime tomorrow. I won't be able to get you the laptop until this weekend, though, but I'll get you a new toothbrush and razor, okay?"

She said, "Okay."

The next day, I stopped at Wendy's and picked up a bacon cheeseburger meal with a Coke. It certainly wasn't the healthiest thing for her to eat, but if she wanted it, why not get it for her? She could certainly indulge all she wanted as far as I was concerned.

I went to the front desk, signed in, and told them I was there to see my mother. I knocked on the door, and Mom was chatting with the same male nurse's aide from the night before. I smiled and said hello to him as I held up the bag of food for her to see and handed her the Coke, which she took and looked happy to have. I took the rolling bedside table that was near her and adjusted it so she could eat from it in bed, and she raised the bed to a more upright position. I unwrapped the sandwich, handed it to her, took out the fries, and placed them on the bag that I put on top of the bedside table.

She seemed content and chatted about the aide after he left. She told me a little bit about him and complained about the lack of channel selection on television. I told her I would bring her the portable DVD player I had bought for the girls to use on the plane trip to Arizona and some of her movies later in the evening so she had something to watch that she liked. The time went by quickly, and she finished her lunch before I left, so I cleaned up the table. I told her, "I'll call you before I come to see if there's anything you want or need."

I returned to work and finished out the day. I did the evening and nighttime routine with the girls, and then I left to see my mother. I had washed her laundry and brought it with me along with the DVD player and a few movies. I called, and she wanted another hamburger. Since McDonald's was the closest fast-food place, I went there after stopping at Walmart to buy her yet another toothbrush and electric razor. I arrived around nine-thirty, and after greeting and signing in at the nurse's station, I went to Mom's room and gave her the food. It was a little late for a meal, but she didn't seem to mind.

I put the DVD player and movies on the chair and put away her clothes in the dresser and the toothbrush in the bathroom. She ate her burger as I showed her the DVD player and how it worked, and she chose to watch the *Star Trek* movie. She asked if I had seen it, and I told her I hadn't.

I cleared the table for her when she finished eating and put the DVD player in the middle so she could watch it more easily. We didn't talk much but sat quietly as she watched the movie, and my mind wandered off to a million different places. After about an hour, a wave of fatigue washed over me, and I told her I was going to go. It was only Tuesday, and I still had to make it through the rest of the week. She put in her order for lunch the next day, another Wendy's burger meal, and I went home.

We visited briefly the next day as she ate her hamburger and told me about the staff in the facility who were nice and the ones who were not. She started to complain a bit about the janitorial staff and how she couldn't understand them. I picked up a hint of paranoia from her discussion about the women. I could see a problem coming down the road. I listened, and after a half hour, went back to work.

Later that night, I went back and put a new movie on for her, and we sat again, mostly in silence, as she watched the movie. She didn't seem to watch anything unless I put it on for her, and despite showing her how to open, close, and turn on/off movies, she didn't seem to be able to do it on her own. This time, I stayed long enough to finish the movie and put on something new for her before I left. At least it would entertain her for a while longer.

The next few days were more of the same. She was starting to struggle a bit more with her ambulation and started to have accidents in the bed. I hadn't really considered she would become incontinent until it happened, at which point I realized how I should have expected that as part of the progression of her decline.

On one of my evening visits, we decided to sit outside on her patio. It was muggy, but tolerable for a late August summer's eve in South Florida. It was almost September now, and my mother had been in South Florida almost a month. Much to my surprise, she still seemed to be doing quite well, all things considered, of course. She started to tell me about her regrets in life and some of the terrible things she had thought and felt—her fears. I let her talk. I knew this to be a stage she needed to go through before being ready to leave. I really didn't want to hear about it, but I sat and listened, playing priest to her confessions. I think she wanted someone to listen, maybe care too, but at least listen.

We sat outside for about an hour and a half, and then we went back inside. I helped her into the bed. "Mom, I can get the computer for you tomorrow, and I can either bring it during the day, but I would have to bring the girls with me, or you can wait until the evening after they've gone to bed."

She answered, "You can bring the girls."

"Okay," I said. "I'll see you in the afternoon then."

The next day, laptop in hand, I knocked on the door and announced, "We're here, Mom." We went in to find her doing what she always was doing, watching television. The girls looked around the room and headed straight for the two empty chairs near the French doors, jumping around as they normally do. I held up the bag with the laptop in it and showed it to my mom as she glared at the girls, looking to decide if she was already annoyed with them.

"I have your laptop, Mom," I said, trying to distract her from my children's presence with her new shiny toy. I plugged in the laptop and placed it on her bedside table. It needed an update, and it was going to take a while. My girls were singing a little bit and were not being exceptionally loud, but in waiting for her computer, my mother was focused on the girls and began to say something to them in an irritated tone of voice.

I cut her off. "I can see you're getting annoyed, so we're going to go now. The computer should finish soon, and you can use it. I'll come back later without the girls to help finish setting it up if you need any help." Before she could say anything more than okay, I turned to the girls and said, "Let's go, girls. Say goodbye to Grandma."

Both of them looked up at their grandmother as she watched them walk past the end of the bed and out the door and they said in unison, "Bye, Grandma." That was the last time the three of them saw each other.

I came back later in the day with some fast-food hamburger meal for her and finished setting up the laptop. I was able to get the password for the hospital's internet and set that up so she could access anything online now. Unfortunately, it worked very poorly, and when I went out, the staff informed me the Wi-Fi didn't work well down that corridor. She could come to the lobby area, and it worked better there.

I helped her out of bed and wheeled her to a desk area in the lobby for people to sit and work on laptops. I helped position her with the computer, and she logged onto her different accounts to check on them. Facebook, banking, etc. She had a rolodex of passwords that she put next to the laptop, and each account had an extensive password that no one could guess. *Ael_!#01faflj_!* She struggled to get into the accounts but was able to do so after awhile and several attempts. After she looked at all the accounts she wanted to, I took her back to her room, lugging the Rolodex, laptop, and Mom in her wheelchair.

We went outside on the porch and watched the sun set behind the bougainvillea, past the water fountain, and beyond the top of the wall where the interstate lay beyond. My mother continued her emotional release, sharing with me her thoughts and feelings that had been held inside her for so long. Some things she told me I could have done without ever knowing, and sadly, I can't say I was entirely surprised by some of the things she confessed. Most of it I don't remember anymore, and what I do remember, I wish that I did not. She was a sick person. I tried to focus on the lovely weather we were having and remain emotion-free and judgment-free to what she divulged.

We sat, she talked, I listened, and the sun faded away. After a couple of hours, I took her back inside the room, closed the French doors, and strained to lift her from the wheelchair and back into bed. I wasn't going to be able to do this much longer. I asked her if she wanted me to pick her up some Depends to wear instead of underwear since she was starting to have trouble getting to the bathroom in time and having accidents.

She blamed the staff for not coming when she used the call button, but regardless of the reason, I knew it wasn't going to get any better, and perhaps she would prefer them. She said, "Yes. Okay," as if giving in.

No one wants to wear adult diapers, but it didn't change that she was now incontinent and couldn't get herself to the bathroom in time to use it. She was only going to decline.

The next day, we sat outside and Mom resumed her confession. I heard her ramble on about all those other regrets, yet not one about me. Today, she focused on me, and I felt conflicted. But on the flip side, I really didn't want to hear it. On occasion, throughout my life, I'd heard the stories about how she hadn't been ready to be a mother and it wouldn't have been a good home for me. She was right. I always knew that, but it didn't change the fact that she wasn't there and left me at the age of three or four. She left and never looked back. It was a reality I lived with every day as a child and was able to put away eventually after I became an adult. It was a long time gone now and didn't matter. She wasn't there for me, end of story.

Maybe she wanted me to say something to her like "It's all right, Mom." Maybe she needed me to give her some gesture that I couldn't give, that I didn't have in me. She started to go down the same droll conversation, and I simply said, "Mom, it's water under the bridge."

She looked at me and, to my surprise, said, "What do you mean?"

I said again, "It's water under the bridge." She still looked at me, puzzled. I continued, not understanding how she didn't know what that saying meant. "It's done. It's over. Don't worry about it." That was the last time we discussed anything related to my childhood. She already said she was sorry, or at least I think she did when I was younger, and it didn't matter anymore. Nothing could change what happened—It was a part of my life, my history. For better or for worse, it was my story that made me who I was whether I like it or not, good or bad.

I visited my mother over lunch the next couple of days, but only once in the evening time. I was fatigued and needed some rest. She seemed situated for the time being, and I opted to only go every other evening unless there was some reason to go more frequently.

She was becoming more agitated and arguing with the staff. As I walked into the facility one evening, I saw one of the nurses who would come in while I was visiting. She was one of the nicer nurses, and I asked her about the nursing home placements. It was going on three weeks now, and they usually placed someone in a home within a month. She told me that nursing home applications had been sent, and I made a list of the names and put it in my purse. I'd call them later in the day to get an idea of where her applications were at in the process. If she were lucky, she would get wait-listed, resulting in her staying longer where she was.

I walked in, and she was upset, complaining about the staff when the doctor and a couple of students with him came to see her. I hadn't met this doctor before. I introduced myself and then sat and listened as he talked with my mother. He assured her the staff there were not out to get her as she complained. Her paranoia was starting to show, and the staff were now getting the full picture of my mother and what I had attempted to get assistance with from them. The doctor told her they would continue her medications, but he would double the dose of her anxiety medication. I didn't ask any questions or say a word. My mother had vilified me to the staff, and she wanted it to stay that way.

The rest of the week and the weekend was more of the same. She had stopped the confessions, though, and I was glad. I think she had come to some sort of peace and a new level of acceptance or readiness for her imminent death. I had no idea what to think when she might pass away. On one hand, I could see her still being around for the holidays and into the new year. I mean, she had already managed to last this long. On the flip side, I could see her decline and would not be surprised if she passed away in the next couple of days.

She was cognitively deteriorating. She would stop mid-sentence and stare blankly at the wall, or she simply wouldn't talk much at all. She would stare ahead with a vacant look in her eyes, and this would go on for a period of time before she'd become alert and resume interactions. Or she would do the opposite and simply fall asleep.

All this time I had waited for this day to come—she wouldn't be so ornery and argumentative, but more docile and amenable. Here it was, and it was so sad to see. I fought back the tears looking at her sitting there oblivious to her surroundings. She was turning another corner in her fight against the cancer, and it was winning. She was starting to succumb to it. She reached the moment I had thought, and to some extent hoped, she would have been at a month earlier when we drove from Arizona to Florida so that it would've been manageable to have her around my children. That hadn't happened, though.

Later, when I called the nursing homes she had been applied to, each one told me they had a wait list of anywhere from nine months to a year and a half, and even one for three years. There was no concern about her getting placed. She would remain at hospice until the end. None of the homes were even close to considering her. So, as long as they didn't reach out to other homes in the area, as there were plenty of them that would take her quickly, but were quite scary, she wouldn't have to worry. She wasn't going anywhere. I didn't have to worry either, at least not for some time now, depending on how much longer she lived.

She was sleeping more now and asleep for a lot of the time I was there, both at lunchtime and in the evenings. Sometimes, I sat the entire time and watched her sleep, seeing if she would wake up. She usually would, and be aware I was there, saying a couple of words, and then I set up *The Golden Girls*, now playing the same disk, as she didn't seem to notice the repetition of the episodes. She could hardly swallow now and wasn't eating most days and barely drinking. She was unable to put a cup with the straw up to her mouth either, and she complained of pain. I thought the end was drawing near.

21

It was Friday, September 16th, and I was in a good mood. I was glad it was the end of the week, and I had the weekend ahead of me. Not so much anything to look forward to, but I didn't have to get up and go to work. I drove to see my mother at lunch, and I didn't expect to find anything other than her asleep in bed. I waved to the staff at the nurse's station as I bypassed the visitor's log at the desk and headed down the corridor to her room. They nodded and smiled back at me. I got to the room, and I heard Mom talking with another nurse, one I had never seen or spoken to before. By now, I pretty much recognized all the staff, and they me.

My mother was alert and rather perky and in a good mood too. She continued to chat with the nurse, and I smiled, happy to see Mom in a good mood and enjoying herself. I told her, "It's nice to see you in a good mood."

She chirped back a quick-witted comeback to me and then said to the nurse, "I love my cranky daughter."

I chuckled. She wasn't wrong about the cranky descriptor for me. I looked at her and said, "And I love my cranky mother."

It was a lighthearted and pleasant visit with my mom. She was her old self and in a good mood. I had to go back to work but stayed a few minutes later than I usually did. I figured if she was in a good mood, I might as well take the time afforded with her, and we chatted for a few minutes after the nurse left.

My mom said, "I really like her."

I was glad she enjoyed her time with the nurse. I told Mom that I would come back and visit that evening, and since she was alert, I asked if there was anything she wanted me to bring.

"I'd really like one of those chocolate malts you brought me before," she said.

I said, "Okay, Mom. I'll bring you a malt." I kissed her on the forehead. "I'll see you later." I was surprised to some extent that she had rebounded like she did, but then it was my mother. If anyone could beat cancer, it was her. It felt like she was finally nearing the end and then miraculously she was back to her old self. I guess it would be a little bit longer, but I was starting to get used to this with her.

When I arrived at the hospital that evening, chocolate malt in hand, it was still somewhat light outside, but it was dusk, and the parking lot lights were already on. I went in, and I was surprised by how eerily quiet it was. I glanced over at the nurse's station as I bypassed it again, and it was all different staff from those who had been there earlier in the day. They didn't pay much notice of me coming.

I headed down the corridor and noticed two of the three workers my mother was paranoid about leaning against the wall speaking quietly yet intently in their conversation. Their conversation stopped as I passed by them. It seemed as if I had interrupted something. I walked a few feet more and could hear the television quite loudly coming from my mother's room. I walked in and saw the third worker standing at the foot of my mother's bed staring at her. It was rather odd the way she was looking at her, and I could only see my mother's feet under the blanket. I continued into the room and could finally see my mother's breathing was quite strained and erratic.

I asked the worker, "What happened?" My mother was obviously in distress, and she was just standing there staring. The worker said nothing and continued to watch her. I yelled at her, trying to take in what was happening to my mom, "Don't stand there. Go get the nurse!"

The worker left at my directive and my mom looked up at me in distress. Her breathing was so belabored. She could not get her breath. I was trying to make sense of what was happening. I shut off the TV so it would be quiet. At first, I wasn't sure what was wrong with her breathing, but it was clear to me it wasn't panic or anxiety. She was simply struggling to breathe.

In the hopes I was wrong, though, I held up the shake and asked, "You don't want the shake, do you?" I knew the answer was no, but I was hoping I was wrong.

She shook her head briefly from side to side, and she was able to blow out a barely audible and breathy "No."

I placed the shake down on the side table as I sat in the chair waiting for the nurse to come. I touched her arm, and she was ice cold. "Mom, are you cold?" She nodded her head, barely able to move it up and down. "Do you want me to put some blankets on you?" She once again struggled to nod her head up and down. I got up and found three blankets in the closet and folded them on top of her to make her as warm as possible. I watched my mother struggle to breathe and asked her if she was in pain. She nodded yes. I asked, "Do you want me to tell the nurse so she can give you some pain medication?" She nodded yes again.

Just then, the nurse came in and, after taking one look, raced over to her on the other side of the bed and started taking her pulse and listening to her heart and breathing. She looked over at me and said, "I'm glad you came when you did." I didn't know what to do or make of this. My mother was not doing well. I asked the nurse if we could turn off the air conditioner because my mother was ice cold. She reached down and felt her arm with the back of her hand and said, "Yes," as she turned around and went to the thermostat on the wall behind her and flipped it off.

I told the nurse my mom nodded yes when I asked her if she was in pain. The nurse hesitated and then looked at my mother who struggled to breathe. I remembered my mother had said she didn't want to be alone, and she didn't want to be in pain. The nurse had my mother's chart with her and said she had hardly received any pain medicine. She didn't have a standing-as-needed order for pain medication, and that surprised the nurse.

She said, "Most patients have a standing order for pain medication. I'll have to call the doctor on call to get an order before I can give her any."

She walked out of the room with the chart in hand, and I stayed sitting in the chair next to the bed. I told my mother, "The nurse is calling the doctor right now so she can give you some pain medication. It'll be a few minutes." I knew the doctor was on-call and would call back quickly. They usually did in these facilities. I watched as my mother continued to breathe with difficulty, not knowing what to say to ease her pain and fear. As I watched her labored breathing, I decided that I would stay the night, even if it meant sitting with her in the chair.

A few minutes passed, and the nurse returned with something for the pain and administered it to her. She said it would take a few minutes to take effect. I looked at Mom and told her

I would be right back. I stepped out into the hall and called to make arrangements for the girls for the night. I hated not putting the girls to bed, but I didn't feel comfortable leaving my mother alone right then.

When I walked back into the room, the nurse was still there, and I told her I would stay the night with her.

The nurse told me, "The doctor gave an order to give her the pain medication every thirty minutes, so if your mom needs more, she can get it in a half hour. If you need anything in the meantime, press the call button." She pointed to it on the other side of the bed. I told her okay, and I sat with my mother, noting the time was nine p.m. She could get more pain medication at nine-thirty. Without realizing it, I found myself holding my mother's right hand which was down by her side on the bed. I was holding it in my right hand tightly as I rubbed her arm with my left hand, trying to comfort her. I found myself lost in thought not saying a word as I stared at her hands.

Suddenly, my mother, still breathing hard and no change in her effort to breathe, twisted her right hand quickly and then back again and one more time with more effort and flung my hand off hers so that I would let go. I stopped for a minute and looked at her trying to breathe and then resumed holding her hand, though not so tightly. I had been squeezing her hand without realizing it. My mother, in one of her final gestures to me, flung my hand off hers. It was a rather poetic gesture that perfectly summarized and captured our entire relationship from beginning to end. Here we were at the end.

It was getting hot in the room, and even with the air conditioner turned off and several blankets piled on top of her, she was ice cold to the touch. She continued to struggle to breathe, and it seemed to slightly worsen. I kept an eye on the clock to ensure she had additional pain medication when the thirty minutes were up. Only ten minutes had passed. I tried to reassure her and said, "In twenty minutes, you can get some more pain medication if you need it, okay?"

As soon as I said it, she seemed to panic, and her breathing became much worse. She breathed so heavily her cheek was being sucked in between her teeth on her right side. Her eyes bulged, and I immediately lunged across her to find the call button for the nurse and pressed it repeatedly. The noise she made gasping for her breath that she could not find was something I had never experienced before.

The nurse came right in and saw her breathing effort and seemed to know it was time. She looked at me and nodded.

I looked at her in bewilderment, trying to wrap my brain around what was happening.

My mother's cheek moved in and out of between her teeth as she sucked her cheek in with each breath she tried to take. Her eyes were wide, and although she was not alone in this moment, I don't think this was what she had wanted it to be like. The nurse stayed as we both watched my mother's cheek move in and out between her teeth. Finally, it stopped after seven minutes of this. I looked at my mom, and her head was turned in my direction, her eyes and mouth wide open. She had stopped breathing. I was still holding her hand.

The nurse felt for a pulse and then listened for a heartbeat with the stethoscope, and after a moment, pulled it away from her chest and said, "She's gone." I turned back to look at my mother, who suddenly gasped for a breath of air. My eyes grew wide with alarm, and I looked back at the nurse who said, "This happens sometimes." I watched the nurse as she repeated the steps and felt for a pulse on my mother's wrist and then listened for a heartbeat with the stethoscope. She said once again, "She's gone." And once again, my mother took in a breath of air with her cheek being sucked in again between her teeth. I turned back to the nurse, who repeated the steps again and again said, "She's gone." I quickly glanced back to my mother, waiting for her to take a final breath once again, but it didn't happen.

The nurse waited a few moments to see if my mom might breathe again, and then said she had to turn the air conditioner back on because of the body. I nodded my head in agreement. I turned to the nurse and said, "Is it alright if I stay in here with her for a little bit?"

She looked at me and replied, "It's fine. I'll be at the nurse's station if you need anything. You can come get me when you're ready."

I shook my head in disbelief that my mother was gone. I can't say I wanted to stay for any reason other than to make sure she was gone. I hated to think I would leave, and she suddenly took another breath a few minutes later. I sat there looking at her. Her eyes were open wide, and it bothered me a bit to see them like that. I really didn't want to touch her since she was dead, I had never touched a dead body before, but I thought perhaps I could close her eyes like they do in the movies so she looked more peaceful.

I hesitated as I reached toward her eyes and after a moment, I tried to run my hand gently over her eyelids to close them, but they didn't close. I only tried once and decided not to try to force it. She lay there, her head turned toward me, her eyes wide open, and her mouth somewhat agape. She was still and quiet. I stayed like that for about a half hour, believing she might take another breath and prolong the end once more, but it never came.

I looked at the chocolate shake sitting on the nightstand and noticed it was completely melted. I grabbed it and tossed it into the garbage can behind me. I walked down the corridor that seemed so brightly lit and out to the nurse's station and asked for the nurse who had been with me when my mom passed away. She was in the chart room documenting what had transpired. My mother passed away at around nine-twenty at night on Friday, September 16, 2011. She was sixty-one years old—three and a half months shy of her sixty-second birthday that I had recently begun to believe she might make it to see.

I told the nurse I was leaving and asked her if I could come back the next day to pick up my mother's belongings. She rather insisted that I take her things then. They had to get the room ready immediately in case it was needed. She said she would help me gather my mother's belongings and I said, "Okay." I backed the minivan to the nearby double doors so we could drop everything in the back of it and I went to my mom's room and gathered her things, and the nurse helped me to pack it all up.

From the bathroom, she grabbed her brush, Sonicare toothbrush, and electric razor and asked me if I wanted them. I told her, "No. Throw them away." I gestured to the garbage can. I went to grab my mother's suitcase from the closet and opened it up to find, sitting in broad daylight another, Sonicare toothbrush and electric razor. I looked at them in disbelief. The toothbrush and razor she accused my daughters of stealing, that I knew they had not, had been placed in her suitcase deliberately. She started that fight that day and had deliberately hidden the toothbrush and razor in her bag. She had gotten me one more time, not an hour after she passed and her body still lying right before me. I tossed the second toothbrush and razor into the garbage can right alongside the other ones the nurse had tossed in.

We continued packing up her stuff. Most of the things I told the nurse to throw away. I quickly emptied the drawers that her clothes were in and tossed them in the bag. I grabbed the faux fiber optic bonsai tree in the cheap plastic fake pot and the framed picture of her father in his younger days she was given at his funeral about five years prior. The nurse put some miscellaneous items in some plastic garbage bags for the stuff that wouldn't fit in the suitcase. I had the rolling case in my hand by the handle. I took one last look around at the room and my mother's still body on the hospital bed.

As we walked to the back of my car and tossed the bags in the trunk, the nurse told me the funeral home had already been called to claim the body and they would be there to take her to the funeral home within a few hours. She gave me the name and number of the home so that I could make the arrangements. I shook my head yes to what the nurse told me, not really processing much. It was drizzling now a very light mist of rain. The nurse turned and headed back into the facility and I got into the car.

It was around ten-thirty, and I drove to the front of the building and pulled into a parking spot. I sat in the car with the windshield wipers on low. I felt numb. Tears pooled in my eyes, and sobs built in my chest. But as I felt the surge of emotions well up and about to burst out of me, they went away. Each time I thought I would explode, the emotions dissipated as quickly as they had built up. I sat for about a half hour before I put the car into reverse, pulled out of the parking lot, and drove home.

When I arrived home, the house was quiet. I sat on the couch. I sat there feeling nothing. I was tired and wanted to go to sleep. I leaned forward, grabbed the remote to the television, and turned it on. I turned it to the Hallmark Channel, and *The Golden Girls* was on. I lay back on the couch in the corner my mother had claimed as her spot a month earlier and closed my eyes, listening to Sophia sass the other women on the show. I fell asleep rather quickly and woke a couple times during the night only to lay there staring out at the stars through the glass doors.

22

My mother had wanted to be cremated, and she had a burial spot back in Arizona. The funeral home here would cremate her and I would take her ashes back to Arizona to be placed in an urn and then interned at her funeral service. I met with the funeral staff later in the week at the crematorium. She was dressed in the dress my mother had with her that I had given them. My mother and I never discussed what she would be cremated in, nor did she leave any directives. I guess because she was to be cremated, she didn't much care one way or the other. However, when I saw the dress, I thought it was appropriate for her. I had brought it in without thinking to iron it, and the guy had told me his wife would take care of it for me.

    A few days later, it was time for her to be cremated. She was in the dress and looked nothing like I knew my mother to look. They had put some makeup on her, and between the makeup and the dress, it looked like a weird version of my mother. I stopped at Field of Flowers on my way to the crematorium and assembled a bouquet of different lilies and some other flowers and added some plastic butterflies to the bouquet. I handed them to the staff to have them placed in the coffin so she had something she liked with her. I knew it was symbolic, but I liked the idea of her being cremated with her favorite flowers and butterflies.

I saw her through the glass as they laid the bouquet on top of her, and the guy gave me a few minutes until I was ready. I looked at her one last time laying in the wooden coffin on the other side of the window. This time, her eyes and mouth were closed. I said nothing and thought nothing as I took in the last moments of my mother's physical presence on this earth. I turned to him and nodded, giving him the go-ahead. He called over to another gentleman that he worked with, and some workers came over and wheeled my mother in her coffin over to the furnace and subsequently into it. A rolling belt moved the coffin from the stand into the furnace. I could see some flames in the furnace, and her body went in, the metal door closed behind and sealed it in the furnace. The staff told me it would take some hours to cremate the body and said he would call me to let me know when I could pick up her ashes.

As I pulled out of the parking lot, I noticed the chimney pipe coming out of the building and the smoke blowing out of it. It was smoke from my mother's furnace, and I thought of it as her spirit leaving this earth as it billowed upward into the sky.

I returned the next day on my lunch break and picked up a cardboard box with a metal box inside it that contained my mother's ashes. Once I returned to Arizona, the staff at that funeral home would transfer her ashes to the urn she had chosen herself earlier in the year. He showed me the paperwork placed in a plastic envelope on the outside of the box that contained the information I would need to give to airline security when I went through the gates.

When I got home, I placed her ashes on the fireplace mantle. The girls and I went and bought a couple bouquets of lilies and placed them in her favorite vase that I now had next to her ashes on the mantle. The flowers lived longer than I expected and lasted until it was time to take her ashes back to Arizona for her funeral.

I took the remaining two days of bereavement leave and flew with her ashes to Arizona and booked a room in a bed-and-breakfast in Sedona with a view of some of the red rocks in the area. I flew into Phoenix, as I had done a little over a month earlier to drive with my mother to Florida, but this time, I was bringing her back to her final resting place. I placed her ashes on the passenger seat along with her favorite hat that she liked to wear when she was hiking. Some fifteen years earlier, she and I had taken a drive from Phoenix to the Grand Canyon and then back through the red rock in Sedona, and it was one of the most stunning places I had ever seen. It seemed fitting to take the drive one last time with her. It was a beautiful drive up, and I listened to her CDs of Native American music, such as R. Carlos Nakai, Tomas Walker, and Nicholas Gunn.

When I arrived at the bed-and-breakfast, I had a beautiful view of Bell Rock from a private patio outside my room. It was so peaceful and quiet. It was not long after I arrived that the sun went down, and I sat outside with my mother's hat on top of her ashes on the table. I had picked up two Corona beers earlier to toast her with. I drank the beers and took in the ambience, feeling her spirit with me.

The next morning, I got up early. I had to drive back to the Phoenix area to drop her ashes so they could be put into the urn prior to her funeral a couple of hours later. But I wanted to drive the scenic view she had introduced me to years ago, so I drove up state road 89A through Oak Canyon from Sedona toward Flagstaff. We had driven that drive in the opposite direction from

Flagstaff to Sedona back toward Phoenix, and we were awestruck by the beauty of the red rock in the area.

Now I drove up the winding road through Oak Creek Canyon. I stopped periodically to take in the views of the different rocks until I finally reached the top. I came upon a cliff where some Native Americans had set up tables and were selling handmade bracelets and other items. Walking around looking at the items, I bought two bracelets I thought my daughters would like. I walked over to the cliff high above Sedona and looked out at the landscape around me. I snapped some pictures of a field of purple flowers behind me, and I headed back down. I would have liked to have spent more time driving in Sedona and around the area, but I had to leave to get the ashes back in time.

I got there right at the time they wanted me to bring her ashes. Part of me felt a loss the moment I handed her ashes to the funeral staff. Others later asked me if I had dumped some of her ashes out on my drive into Sedona, but I didn't. Personally, the thought of touching someone's ashes was as gruesome a prospect as, well, trying to close her eyes after she passed away. I didn't even open the metal box that contained her ashes. I had no desire or interest in doing so. I was somewhat insulted that they thought that I could do something like that, but it's something my mother might have well done had the roles been reversed.

After I took her ashes at the funeral home, I had a couple of hours to pass until the funeral would start, so I drove one last time up South Mountain like I had done nine months earlier while my daughters napped in the back of the car. I looked out over the city of Phoenix from atop the mountain, remembering how far I had come in those last nine months. My lip quivered and everything came rushing at me, but as before, as quickly as the emotions built, I held them back and stuffed them down.

As the time neared for her funeral, I headed down the mountain and made my way back to the funeral home. As soon as the funeral began, the tears flowed down my face. Decades of pent-up feelings unleashed at once. I could not contain the emotions any longer. I sobbed quietly until her ashes, now in the blue urn, were interned into their final resting place with a slight view of a mountain. The tears stopped as soon as it was over, and I drove back to Sedona for the remainder of the day. I went to a Mexican restaurant in the area, as my mother would have wanted, and took a hike in Red Rock State Park. I spent the evening once again on the patio watching the sun go down over Bell Rock, drinking a couple of Corona beers, this time wearing my mother's Stetson-styled hat with the feather sticking out of it.

23

September 16, 2021

It's been ten years now since my mother passed away. I awoke at five in the morning, and while momentarily weighing the option of closing my eyes and falling back to sleep, I opted to get out of bed. I drove the forty minutes to the beach as the sun was lighting the sky with lovely pink, peach, and yellow hues beyond the clouds on the ocean horizon. The waves were almost non-existent, a rarity for the ocean, rather tranquil and calm. From the parking lot, I descended stairs to the sand below. I slipped my flip-flops off at the wall and trekked my way along the water. The waves rolled in and out, soaking the bottoms of my capris below the knees.

I played Tomas Walker's "Soaring" from his album *Spirit Dreams*, which I inherited from my mother some ten years earlier. I felt the serenity of the somber flute belting into my ears via my corded earbuds tethered to my phone in my pants pocket. I headed north as the horizon illuminate brighter and brighter while passing the periodic passerby. I found the song almost hypnotic in its transcendence and the sun broke through the hidden clouds, ascending the ocean line on the horizon. It was almost prophetic to watch as I imagined releasing my mother's spirit from me at that very moment. I turned, having walked far enough, and headed back south down the beach, putting on my own music after finishing "Soaring."

Afterward, I climbed back in my car and headed directly west and found myself at the light I had sat at those ten years earlier so many times, turning to visit my mother, and the final time to watch my mother take her last breath.

I hadn't planned on stopping, but impulsively, I pulled into the parking lot of the hospice, backed my car into a spot near where my mother's room had been, and pressed the hands-free button on the steering wheel, asking Siri to play "Don't Fear the Reaper" by Blue Öyster Cult. My mother played this album on our drive from Arizona to Florida, her final destination. I chuckled as I listened to it, watching the sun begin to light the building in front of me. The song seemed to end in a flash. I placed the car in drive and pulled away, passing what appeared to be a security guard exiting the double-sliding glass doors to the entrance to the facility I exited ten years prior. He watched me as I pulled out of the driveway and left the vicinity.

I'm now fifty instead of forty, and a little over ten years younger than she was when she passed away. So much has happened in the past decade since she departed this earth. I often think of how she would have handled or reacted to what has happened these ten years. How many people would she have yelled at saying, "You're going to die," when she saw them not social distancing or wearing a mask during this pandemic. Or would she have felt otherwise? I dare think not, but Marion was an enigma and should not be underestimated.

My children are teenagers now, the days of youth are far behind me, and I don't think about my mother as much as I used to. I can't say I have truly processed everything we went through together in my forty years, much less that final year. I write this to share my story and to finally let go of what I have not been able to. I realize some things in life stay with us forever, and as far as my mother is concerned, that final year will be what I recall most about her, and it will stay with me forever.

I am regretful my mother could never let go and move on with her life, that it was so sad and hard for her. I wish she had been able to find peace with her getting pregnant with me and not let it halt her life, carrying that guilt, shame, regret, anger, and whatever other emotions she always had about it. Right or wrong, I was the catalyst that threw her life out of whack, and she could never get past it. I can only hope that through me and through my children, her spirit somehow will live on and that she has found peace in death that eluded her in life and the freedom from her past that haunted and shackled her during her days on this earth.

I have a hopeful image of her spirit flying free once it was released into the sky and floating high above in the Sonoran Desert above the cacti and red rock as she soars amongst the chemtrails in the cloudless Arizona sky.

I love you, my cranky mom.

May you truly rest in peace.

-Your cranky daughter

www.ingramcontent.com/pod-product-compliance
Lightning Source LLC
Chambersburg PA
CBHW071712090426
42738CB00009B/1752